MONTANA STATE'S
GOLDEN BOBCATS

MONTANA STATE'S GOLDEN BOBCATS

1929 BASKETBALL NATIONAL CHAMPIONS

PAUL R. WYLIE

Published by The History Press
Charleston, SC
www.historypress.com

Copyright © 2022 by Paul R. Wylie
All rights reserved

Front cover, top left: Max Worthington, guard for the 1928–29 "Golden Bobcats" basketball team. *Top center*: From left to right: Orland Ward, Frank Ward and John Ashworth "Cat" Thompson. *Top right*: John "Brick" Breeden, guard for the 1928–29 "Golden Bobcats" basketball team. *Bottom*: Montana State's Golden Bobcat basketball team of 1928–29. Back row, from left to right: Clifford Swanson (manager), Ed Buzzetti, John "Brick" Breeden (guard), Captain Frank Ward (center), "Max" Worthington (guard), Harold Sadler and Schubert Dyche (coach). Front row, from left to right: Fred "Red" Browning (guard), Ott Gardner, Tommy "Cat" Thompson (forward), Orland Ward (forward), "Peck" McFarland and Roy Homme. *Back cover*: New gymnasium on the Montana State campus, 1923. *Insert*: Ott Romney.

All photos courtesy Montana State University, Special Collections.

First published 2022

Manufactured in the United States

ISBN 9781467150415

Library of Congress Control Number: 2021952412

Notice: The information in this book is true and complete to the best of our knowledge. It is offered without guarantee on the part of the author or The History Press. The author and The History Press disclaim all liability in connection with the use of this book.

All rights reserved. No part of this book may be reproduced or transmitted in any form whatsoever without prior written permission from the publisher except in the case of brief quotations embodied in critical articles and reviews.

The 1929 Golden Bobcats. *Montana State University*.

CONTENTS

Acknowledgements	9
Introduction	11
1. John Ashworth "Cat" Thompson: Also Known as Ashworth Thompson, "Tommy" Thompson and Even Better Known as "Cat" Thompson, All-American Basketball Player	13
2. George Ottinger "Ott" Romney	23
3. Ott Romney Comes to Montana State as a Player	27
4. Onward to Billings: Ott Romney Becomes a Coach	32
5. The Great War	35
6. MSC Gets a New President and a New Gym	39
7. Schubert Reilly Dyche	44
8. The Development of Basketball in the United States	49
9. Ott Romney's Early Years as Montana State's Coach	51
10. Ott Romney Builds a Team at Montana State	54
11. John William "Brick" Breeden	56
12. The 1925–26 Bobcats: The Beginning of the Future	59
13. The Brothers: Frank Ward and Orland Ward of Parowan, Utah	65
14. The Recruiting of the Golden Bobcats	72
15. Trip to Montana	79
16. 1926–27 Season	83

Contents

17. Max Worthington	89
18. 1927–28 Season: Putting the Championship Team Together	94
19. The 1928 Conference Season	102
20. Ott Romney Leaves His Team after the 1928 Season	111
21. 1928–29 Season: Stand Up and Cheer	116
22. The Bobcats Grieve over a Teammate's Death and Almost Lose Max Worthington to Rheumatic Fever	119
23. The Cook Painters Come to Town	122
24. The Best of the Championship Season: "A Collection of Artists"	130
25. The National Championship Postseason	138
26. Decision Time for Cat Thompson	140
Epilogue	143
Notes	145
Bibliography	159
Index	165
About the Author	173

ACKNOWLEDGEMENTS

Certainly not as far back as 1929, but in my childhood years in the 1940s and early 1950s, I have memories of meeting members of the 1929 Golden Bobcat team and particularly Max Worthington, a Wylie family friend who visited our home frequently. I kept in touch with Max right up to his passing in 1993, and we often talked basketball, giving me a privileged insight into the team—who they were and how they played. Doug Worthington, Max's son, was someone I have known since I was young, and he, too, has been able to provide me with much detail.

Sons and daughters of the other players were very helpful in my research, and I can't give enough thanks to them. Devon Sanderson and his wife, Judy, who is "Cat" Thompson's daughter, have done a monumental job of putting together a memorial collection for Cat that includes newspapers, articles, a biography, personal recollections and even a sound recording of Cat talking about his life and his basketball career. They have graciously provided me with this material. Ruth Breeden Cegelski, Bill Breeden and Tom Breeden, who are Brick Breeden's children, have given me much information. I was pleasantly surprised to find that Orland Ward's son Tex had been a close childhood friend while growing up in Laramie, Wyoming, of my next-door neighbor Ralph Lindahl, who put me in touch. Tex provided me with valuable information that filled in a lot of the blanks.

Early in my research, I stopped through Parowan, Utah, looking for information on Frank Ward and his family. Jet Smith of the visitor center there was kind enough to put me in touch with Gale Stulk. As star player

Acknowledgements

Frank Ward's nephew, Gale gave me great family information and referred me to his daughter Wendy Lisonbee in Paradise, Utah who with her husband, John, provided me with old family photos and more information. Historians at centers in La Verkin, St. George, Cedar City and Parowan have been of great help, as have the librarians at Utah State University in Logan and the University of Utah in Salt Lake City. At Montana State University, historian Bill Lamberty, who is in charge of athletic publicity, has been a great friend and supplied valuable information. Kim Allen Scott, who is no longer at the MSU Library, did a great job of pointing me in the right directions. Gary Barnhart, in charge of photos there, has given me great help. The registrar's office at MSU has been of great help in finding and providing historical transcripts.

After graduating from MSC in 1930, Frank Ward, together with his wife, Mary, and their two boys, Jim and Hal, stayed in Montana. In the 1950s, when I was on a high school basketball team, Frank was the coach of a team we were playing. Like many coaches did in those days, he came over to our bench to shake hands with me and my teammates. I remembered him as an impressive man and a good coach who got the most out of his team. Brick Breeden had a career as a coach and administrator at Montana State and was running the MSU career placement service at the time I graduated. He was well known to the Wylie family, particularly by my uncle Gus Wylie, who played with him when he was on the football team both in high school and college. Vallery Glynn was on the team until a year before the 1929 championship year, and I knew him later as dean of students when I was in college. I have been friends with his son Marty for a long time. Marty has supplied valuable information. I owe many thanks to my wife, Arlene Wylie, my daughter, Lynne Catherine Wylie, and my sons, John and Tom Wylie, for their help and encouragement in this project.

My thanks also to editors Artie Crisp and Rick Delaney at The History Press for their fine work.

—Paul R. Wylie
Bozeman, Montana, September 15, 2021

INTRODUCTION

On Sunday morning, January 27, 1929, the sports fans of Provo, Utah, woke to an article written by a Montana sports reporter telling them that the local BYU Cougars basketball team had just suffered an embarrassing loss, 67–37, in Bozeman, Montana.[1] The Bobcats of Montana State had beaten BYU and their coach, Ott Romney. The irony was that Romney had been beaten by the team and the players he had recruited in Utah to come north to Montana State, where he had coached until the year before. What had gone wrong here, the Utah fans asked![2]

Later that year, the "Golden Bobcats," as they ended up being called, would surprise the nation by being designated national collegiate champions, with Utah natives Frank Ward and Cat Thompson named All-Americans.

This is the story of how the Golden Bobcat team came to be.

1

JOHN ASHWORTH "CAT" THOMPSON

Also Known as Ashworth Thompson, "Tommy" Thompson and Even Better Known as "Cat" Thompson, All-American Basketball Player

"Tommy" Thompson who is known on the basketball floor as "Cat" for very good reasons, has earned for himself the reputation of being the greatest forward in the West, and one of the four top-notchers of the nation.
—Montana State College 1929 Montanan *yearbook*

What you persist in doing becomes easy for you to do, not that the nature of the thing has changed, but your ability to do it has increased.
—Heber J. Grant [3]

In August 1926, it was very hot in the southern Utah country town of La Verkin. There, a wiry twenty-year-old John Ashworth "Cat" Thompson was working in the plowed fields of his family's farm on the outskirts. He interrupted what he was doing when he saw a car putting up a cloud of dust coming toward him. It had an out-of-state license plate from far north Montana, and when it came to a stop, a disheveled, travel-weary man stepped out. Ashworth recognized him as Schubert Dyche, someone he had talked to casually just once before. This time, the traveler wanted to talk to him about something very serious. It was basketball.

The dry plateau where the two men were meeting was cut by a deep ravine with Utah's Virgin River running far below. From high upstream in the canyon, water flowed both in the main channel and down the elevated Hurricane Canal, which clung to the canyon wall. It had been blasted and dug to bring water from seven miles upstream to be let out on the tableland above the ravine. The small town of Hurricane to the south of the chasm and La Verkin to the north were within just a short distance of each other, connected by a wooden bridge across the ravine allowing horses, wagons and pedestrians to go back and forth.⁴

Ashworth Thompson's parents were among the first descendants of the Mormon pioneers coming to the area under the leadership of Erastus Snow, who had been sent by Brigham Young. They were there to develop lands suitable for raising cotton. The grim-faced pioneers would soon see that the cotton they were planning to grow could indeed flourish in a dry climate, but they needed irrigation water, and so the Hurricane Canal was constructed. It took years to build, but the intrepid Mormons

Cat Thompson. *Montana State University*.

kept after it. They believed that a "successful solution" to the aridity barring their farming "was the price of their existence." As they were told, "all should work for what they were to have, and that all should have what they had worked for."

With expectations that the canal would be completed at some time, a few of the pioneers platted out the town of La Verkin and settled in to scratch out a decades-long existence until the water would arrive. It was a slow process. Not until September 1893 was a company formed to work out the details of the digging that Snow had envisioned. In time, the monumental effort was completed, and in April 1904, water was turned into the canal in time for spring planting on the bench.⁵

The biggest settlement in the area was St. George, Utah, some twenty miles to the west of La Verkin over rock-strewn roads. In 1861, it had been founded as Mormon pioneer Erastus Snow's cotton mission and had been called Dixie by Brigham Young. Cotton was never produced at competitive market rates, and in time, the crop was abandoned in favor of others as the pioneers settled in permanently.⁶ The settlers included Cat's father and mother, who had both attended school in St. George, where his father, Wilford, was an outstanding athlete. He and Kate Judd were married in a ceremony solemnized in the Mormon temple there. In La Verkin, where they lived, Wilford practiced the trades he had learned as a painter and paperhanger until he got a small amount of dry land and settled down to a life of farming, family and church, The Church of Jesus Christ of Latter-day Saints (LDS).

Less than two years after the canal's completion, Wilford and Kate Thompson found themselves making a buggy trip, which, despite their hurry, seemed to be an eternity over a rocky pass and down a canyon to St. George. Once there, on February 10, 1906, Wilford's grandmother Dr. Elizabeth Perkes Thompson delivered a baby named John Ashworth Thompson. By custom, his first name was not used, and he grew up as Ashworth Thompson. Later, he would be called "Tommy" Thompson, and still later, after he had achieved national fame as one of the best basketball players in the country, he was universally called "Cat" Thompson for his feline quickness. It was a name that stuck for the rest of his life.

As he was growing up, Cat Thompson became an extra set of hands on his father's farm, and he learned to prune grapevines and peach trees; plow; cut, rake and haul hay; clean ditches; and pick fruit. It was hard work but rewarding, because Cat knew he was helping his family survive—a hard endeavor in a hard country.[7] Even with the never-ending work, there was still time for sports, and baseball was first to draw his attention. He watched the older men—athletes like his father—hit pitches and run around bases on the hard-packed dirt of the city square, sometimes taking the skin off their elbows as they slid into base. The competition was intense, and none of the men wanted to lose, particularly against the team that had crossed the bridge from Hurricane bringing their civic pride and attitudes with them. In the hot, high desert climate, the competition went on all year, and the young boys, even as little tykes, took up the pastime as soon as they could shoulder a bat or pitch a ball somewhere in the vicinity of the plate.

Then there was the dawning of a new day. A new game had crowded its way in and took over Cat's life forever. Soon after he started grade school in a one-room mud and plaster building in the center of town, he became fascinated by basketball. To make it possible to play on the dirt playground where the students of all ages took their recesses together, the city fathers raised two sturdy poles to which were attached backboards of lumber and iron rings as hoops. The games quickly started.

Ashworth soon found out that the competition was intense. The gentler attitudes of the LDS Church were set aside as the boys pushed

Bridge over the Virgin River in Utah. Cat Thompson grew up in arid farm country in horse-and-buggy days. The men on the town teams and the boys on the grade-school teams from La Verkin, and Hurricane would cross the bridge to play one another in baseball and basketball. Date unknown. *Utah Historical Society*.

and shoved their way to get whatever advantage they could under the basket, even if it resulted in bloody noses and deep bruises. The goal was to get the frequent rebounds at any cost so that the ball could be shot again in kind of a toss, fling or push that were the skills of the time, only to miss again, and again, until finally the ball would miraculously go into the basket. It was rough and required stamina, quickness and bravery, and young Thompson, one of the smallest kids, had it all.

As the La Verkin boys got older, basketball competition started in earnest against the boys from Hurricane. Winning at all costs was vitally important to preserve the honor of the town. The games were played in a swirl of dust, stirred up by the players' shoes on the packed dirt. The stitched leather basketball, when bounced, would leave little, almost unseen, depressions in the hard pack, along with some fine dirt particles. It was a grimy sport as the dirt mixed with sweat and dried to form a glaze on bare skin. It would not be washed off until the weekly Saturday-night bath in a laundry tub with water warmed in the reservoir on the side of the wood-burning kitchen stove. Sometimes, the La Verkin boys, tired, dirty and sweaty, went down the steep gorge to the Virgin River to go skinny dipping. There was no need for swimsuits, and there were none to be had anyway, so what difference did it make? It was all part of pioneer life in Utah.

As a student, John Ashworth "Cat" Thompson learned well what was taught in La Verkin's small school, and he learned basketball; the boys played on the playground night after night, sometimes by the light of the moon.[8] Even in this rough world, he was acquiring lifetime skills. In a school where the younger boys played with the older, taller players, he had to suffer having his shots blocked time and again and, in the process, getting knocked down. Crawling to his feet without a whimper, he became determined to find a way to get a shot off. The ball had to go over, through or around the wall of arms and bodies that appeared in front of him, and Ashworth set out to find which way was best.

To get past the bigger boys, he tried dribbling the ball, but it was almost out of the question. The early basketballs comprised stitched leather coverings over a rubber bladder that had a protruding inflation pipe, covered by bulky laces. The ball would be thrown off at strange angles if it struck the wrong way. Stepping through the spaces between the larger defenders between Ashworth and the basket was also out of the question, as the bulky boys were usually packed together in an impenetrable wall. Finally, after months of practice, Ashworth found his way. He could actually shoot the ball with one hand—almost a hook shot, something not many did in those days. At least he was able to get the shot off, and sometimes the defenders could only look at the ball falling through the hoop.

Young Thompson had been out playing basketball one day when he noticed a tall man with a commanding presence watching the game. Heber J. Grant, the president of the LDS Church, was there observing, and his intelligent eyes reflected his own history of determination. As he watched the young boys shooting the basketball, his experience told him that there was at least one young player whose abilities would put him on the road to success if he made hard demands on himself and kept practicing. That boy was later introduced to Grant as John Ashworth Thompson.

Grant's message, when he spoke to the LDS congregation that day, was heard plainly by all, and it was almost as if it was personally directed at Ashworth. "What you persist in doing becomes easy for you to do, not that the nature of the thing has changed, but your ability to do it has increased." Ashworth heard Grant's message, believed in it and decided simply and without hesitation that he wanted to be the best basketball player in the world. As soon as the meeting was over, Cat went back to the playground and practiced until late at night. Even though he was growing up to be a not very tall person, it never occurred to him that he might not be tall enough for basketball. To him, it didn't matter, because he had already found a way to shoot over taller defenders. It was his success on the court that counted, and the primary measure of that success to him would always be the scoring of baskets.

Another thing Cat learned to do in the long days of practice to come was to concentrate on the trajectory of the ball on open shots, and he came to believe that his shots, put up with either one hand, the left or the right, or two hands, should be arched. "You don't shoot at the basket." As he said, "you lay the arch up in the air out in front of the basket, and if you do a good job of arching, the ball will fall in the basket. If you shoot at it, why you're hitting it too hard or it's going too far or the like." He eventually developed a shot that in later years would be referred to as the "tear drop": he would glide through the air and release the ball in a gentle arch some distance from the basket. If he missed, his tremendous leaping ability was good for getting his own rebound.[9]

On regular trips to visit Ashworth's grandparents in St. George, the family could not help but notice a new schoolhouse going up. They saw the volcanic rock base put in place and pink, locally quarried sandstone walls rising three stories. It was the new home for the then two-decade-old Dixie Academy, sponsored by the LDS Church. Already there was talk about Ashworth going to school there when he was ready.[10] It became a subject of no small interest to the Thompson family, and they learned in 1916 that two years of a teacher's college curriculum had been added in the same school building. That year, the program was named Dixie Normal College. But this news didn't mean anything to Ashworth. What was impressed on his mind was the large brick building going up next to the academy. It was a gymnasium with a basketball court, and the gleaming, varnished oak floors and incandescent overhead lights held magical promise for the youngster.

When Cat graduated from the eighth grade, neither La Verkin nor neighboring Hurricane had a high school. The only option his family had to get secondary education for Ashworth was to board him in St. George, but they couldn't afford it. For a time, it looked like he would stay home and work, until the question was brought up to Kate's parents. They were getting older and in need of some help, and it was decided that young Ashworth

1929 Basketball National Champions

Dixie High School and Junior College in St. George, Utah. *Courtesy Dixie State University Library Photo Archives.*

would live with them and do some much-needed work around their house and attend Dixie High School during the day. It worked out well for all. Cat did things like cooking the midday meal on his noon hour away from school and helping his grandfather with baths. Cat had a nice room in their house, and it was not far to school, where he took up playing basketball indoors for the first time in his life.

The first two years at Dixie High School were fun ones for young Thompson. He missed his family in La Verkin, but he was getting better at basketball, and that was what he wanted the most. He was thrilled to join the Dixie squad, despite having to shoulder the indignity of being on the second team the first year. Even with his unusual shooting skills, Cat was not yet a total player, mostly because the hard-packed dirt courts in La Verkin had not given him a chance to dribble, which he now started to learn on the hardwood. In his sophomore year, he thought his chances were good for making the first team, but at Christmastime, while trying one of his off-balance shots, he sprained his ankle and missed out again on being a starter. It wasn't until his junior year that he became a standout on the high school basketball team.[11] [12] Cat Thompson was starting to get a hint of bigger things in sports, and the more attention he got, the better he performed. In St. George, things got a little more complicated when, after Cat had been in her home for two years, Cat's grandmother died. He had to move in with another family in town, doing chores for them while he finished attending Dixie High School.[13]

There was no doubt in those days that the basketball teams from the big schools up north in the Great Salt Lake, Utah and Cache Valleys considered the Dixie High School squad a country team—the "hicks from the sticks," they said. Thompson and the rest of the players there knew that when it came time to go up north to the state tournament, they would have to put up with some derision. "When you're from the sticks you're nobody—and those guys from the big cities would just like to cram it down our neck," one of the players said. Instead of ignoring the jeers, they decided to take some action. When the coach put in a new scheme, the players would play it to the hilt to get attention. The Dixie player who had the ball would yell out in a loud voice "All Around Shep!," and all of a sudden the four other players would run back and forth through the defense, crisscrossing and winding from one side of the court to the other. The other team's astonished players stood frozen in disbelief, turning their heads and wondering what was going on, failing to guard anyone. When Dixie's tallest player came open under the basket, the guard would throw the ball to him, usually for a score. "All Around Shep" didn't really mean anything, but they had to call it something, and it got in the face of the city boys.

Basketball prowess had already become one of the things sought after in Utah, and particularly at Dixie. In 1923, the Dixie five narrowly missed the state championship. It was only by 1 point in a game, but the humbling experience long stayed on Cat's mind. For a time afterward, he thought of nothing else but avenging the loss, which he did. As he told it: "Our Dixie basketball team did win the Utah State tournament. One night I was lucky and scored a state record, 56 points, which stood up for many years." Coach Chester Whitehead took the team on to Chicago to the National Interscholastic Tournament at the University of Chicago, where teams from all over the country competed. Little Dixie High School played six games in five days at the event and won the consolation trophy, having been barely beaten by the championship team. It was a moral victory and erased the memory of the 1-point loss the previous year in the state high school tournament.[14]

Following his high school graduation in 1924, Ashworth moved on to continue his education as one of the sixty or so students at Dixie College, as well as to play basketball. Records indicate that he played there in both the 1925 and 1926 seasons. It wasn't much of a move, because he had the same coach and the same gym as he had in high school, but it kept him playing and working toward getting on a team from one of Utah's three universities. Ashworth said: "My freshman year at Dixie College, was a good year. I gained much needed experience, worked hard, and practiced with a desire to be good enough to go to a larger college the next year. A dream and hard work was to bring me this big opportunity."[15]

Despite his efforts and his success at Dixie College, all he really had to look forward to was more work on his family's farm. None of the Utah colleges had shown much interest. He learned later that his stint at Dixie Junior College might count against his college eligibility and that the Utah colleges preferred only four-year players. At least that was the rumor. It looked like he would not get his opportunity to go to a larger school. As luck would have it, all of that changed by the end of the summer of 1926, when the car with the Montana license plate, trailed by its cloud of dust, pulled up and Schubert Dyche stepped out to talk basketball.

After reintroducing himself, Schubert immediately got down to business. It seemed an almost improbable proposition, and Schubert had some questions. Would Ashworth be interested in coming to Bozeman, Montana, to go to college and play basketball with the Montana State Bobcats under head coach Ott Romney? Of course Cat was interested! He was now twenty years old and of an age when he had to plan for the future. He wanted it to include both basketball and college. But how many years would he be allowed to play?

Schubert Dyche picked up on Thompson's concern and was prepared to answer it. Romney had told him about his meeting with President Atkinson, and he had passed on the solution to Schubert. The offer Ashworth heard was simple. Schubert asked him if he would have any objection to enrolling as a freshman and starting his college career over again, if—and it was a big if—he could play for four years. Ashworth thought about that for all of a few minutes before he agreed. Just a few details had to be worked out. Thompson said: "I told him I would go but would need a job to help me through. He agreed and said he would send a car for me in the fall. The summer went fast. I worked and dreamed of the future at Montana State College."[16]

With that behind him, Schubert turned his attention to Frank Ward, the talented center of the Branch Agricultural College (BAC) junior college basketball team in Cedar City, only about fifty miles to the north of La Verkin. By this time, Ashworth and Frank, as the two best players in southern

Utah, were well acquainted, having played against each other. Cat had not heard that Frank intended to enroll and play basketball at any of the three Utah college teams. There was some thought that Frank might not want to continue playing because, as someone who would soon be twenty-three, he thought he might be too old. He was married and had a one-year-old child. Schubert knew the level of Frank's abilities and thought it worth a try anyway. As Schubert headed north out of La Verkin toward Montana on his way home, he hoped to talk to Frank in either Cedar City or Parowan and get him interested in coming to Montana State. He succeeded.[17]

After Shubert Dyche's visit, Thompson's summer wore on, seemingly endlessly. He was getting a little nervous. That is, until one hot afternoon in late August, when he was pulling in from his father's field with a load of hay on a horse-drawn cart. There was a strange car in front of the house. The driver introduced himself as Joe Ottenheimer, the student athletic manager from Montana State College. He had come to drive Cat to Montana. "How soon can you be ready?" Joe asked. A quick reply came from Thompson: "As soon as I change clothes, maybe 30 minutes."[18]

2

GEORGE OTTINGER "OTT" ROMNEY

[There] must be a lot of drill sergeant in a coach....Although he lives on drill, drill, drill—drive, drive, drive—scheme, scheme, scheme—and excitement and adulation. The limelight forever plays on him. Sometimes, it singes him. He is alternately the public's darling and the public's scapegoat. His weekends are successive Armageddons. He is apt to acquire a tender ego, dyspepsia and jittery nerves.
—Ott Romney, Off the Job Living[19]

In the fall of 1926, Coach Ott Romney waited tentatively on the Montana State College campus in Bozeman. Automobiles were to arrive from Utah. They would bring Frank Ward and Ashworth Thompson. Maybe they would be just the players he needed for the next four years. Time would tell. Ott was relieved when Joe Ottenheimer showed up in his car, driving Thompson. At about the same time, another car pulled in, driven by Frank Ward and carrying his wife and baby boy. Along with them had come Frank's younger brother Orland Ward, who had finished playing basketball at Parowan High School. Orland's arrival was somewhat of a surprise to Ott and viewed initially as a challenge, because Orland did not have the athletic reputation of his older brother. Ott would have to find a place for him on his freshman team—unless he was an inept player, which he likely was not. Above all else, Frank had to be kept happy.

Romney had been the coach at Montana State College for several years, but he was not from Montana. He was from Utah, where he had been

Ott Romney. *Montana State University.*

born into the large Romney family in Salt Lake City in the Utah Territory. That was in 1892, four years before Utah's statehood. It was the same year that the University of Deseret, founded in 1850 in Salt Lake City by church leader Brigham Young, became the University of Utah. That was just three years after the Mormon pioneers came to the Salt Lake Valley in 1847 after escaping religious persecution that had driven them out of Illinois and Missouri.[20]

Romney took his first and middle names from his maternal grandfather, George M. Ottinger.[21] Instead of being known as "George," his family wanted him called "Ott," a name he used his entire life. He was the oldest of five scrappy brothers renowned for their athletic abilities. Even as children they were famous for the intensity of their games in Salt Lake City's prestigious, tree-lined lower avenues.

The Romney boys were raised with the intense desire to win competitions, including those against each other. Footraces, jumping, basketball, football, tennis and less formal games such as kick the can—or kick the other guy in the shins, as it sometimes became. They also had boxing, which might be just fistfights when gloves weren't available. For basketball, they used hoops attached to the sides of barns and garages. For football, they used any ball they could find, and for protection against hard physical contact, Ott had homemade pads sewn into his jersey. For tennis and baseball, wooden rackets and bats milled at the local lumberyard were sanded down at home. Bloodied noses were routine; bruised shins were suffered in silence as a sign of pride for surviving the battles. One Christmas, the five Romney brothers were given boxing gloves. The gifts were accompanied by gauze and bottles of liniment.[22]

In later years, Ott Romney could look back on his early life with satisfaction and pride. Most of the neighborhood families were neither rich nor poor, but they uniformly worked hard in the Mormon tradition and competed hard in all endeavors. The community had produced all-conference and All-American athletes, a circus performer for the Ringling Brothers show, a Rhodes scholar, doctors, lawyers, a Broadway actress, college professors and professional bicycle riders. His own brother became a professional football player. That was to say nothing of national politics. Ott's cousin George W. Romney became Michigan's governor, and George's son and former Massachusetts governor Mitt Romney ran for president of the United States.[23]

The next oldest boy was Earnest Lowell "Dick" Romney, three years Ott's junior, who became a four-sport star at the University of Utah. A third brother, Milton "Mitt" Romney, was known as the "Utah Flash" and played at first for Utah, where he was an All–Rocky Mountain Conference halfback as a freshman. Then Amos Alonzo Stagg recruited him to play for the University of Chicago, which in its early years was one of the nation's leading universities for both academics and sports. In 1922, he went on to lead his team to the Big 10 football championship as a senior quarterback before going on to the NFL, where he played quarterback for the Chicago Bears from 1925 to 1928. W.W. "Woody" Romney, the fourth brother, lettered in football at Utah and was captain of the 1919 basketball team. Floyd Romney, the fifth brother, lettered for two seasons at Utah and then followed his brother Ott to Montana State, finishing his athletic career there.[24]

It was natural for Ott to want to play sports at the University of Utah. He had dreamed of competing for the Utes and playing against the LDS Church–sponsored Brigham Young University, just forty miles to the south in Provo. He attended the Utah home basketball games, which were played in the church's Deseret Gym, an imposing structure of classical architecture near the LDS temple. Along with the noisy crowd, the youngster Ott cheered the team on to mostly victories; he suffered with the team and its fans when they lost. Through it all, he became a Ute in his heart. One player he admired in particular was the tall, athletic Fred Bennion, an all-conference fullback. After Bennion graduated, he became the young coach of the Utes, and Ott played for him.[25] That would not be the end of the association of Ott Romney and Fred Bennion.

As an eighteen-year-old freshman, not yet fully developed, Ott backed up his cousin Lon Romney at halfback before becoming the starter at quarterback toward the end of the season. When basketball season came, he made the varsity team and contributed immediately to the Utes' success. During the year, he matured and added strength and weight, and by the time football season rolled around the next fall, it became clear he would be one of the top players. He was first positioned at fullback, even though his starting position was listed as end, where his running ability was used on numerous end-around and reverse plays. His strength and speed stood out and earned him all-conference honors.

Ott's life at the University of Utah involved more than just athletics. He joined the Sigma Chi social fraternity in 1910, but it wasn't just that which earned him membership in the university's Beehive Club in 1913. It was the highest award given to senior students and was based on "scholarship, leadership, and effective contributions to the campus through student activities."[26] By the end of the football season in 1912, it was announced that he would be graduating in the spring after three years. He had been accepted to Harvard University the next academic year. He left Utah with a year of eligibility remaining. Under Harvard's rules, Ott was not eligible for major sports the next year, so he had nothing to do but concentrate on his studies, which he completed by midyear. He returned to the University of Utah but, having already graduated, was no longer eligible to play. He continued with the team as a student assistant.[27]

3

OTT ROMNEY COMES TO MONTANA STATE AS A PLAYER

Ott Romney, who formerly was a football star at the university of Utah is said to have been hired as an assistant coach at the Bozeman Agricultural College.…If this is true he is automatically thrown into the professional ranks and can occupy no place on a college athletic team.
—Salt Lake City Telegram, *October 6, 1914*[28]

The 1910s in Montana opened with the renewal of an old argument between then Montana State University in Missoula and Montana State College (MSC) in Bozeman. Missoula seemed to favor the consolidation of the two schools. In Bozeman, President James Hamilton wanted his college to remain a separate unit in order to fulfill the dream of having it become another Massachusetts Institute of Technology (MIT). As dreary as that may have sounded to the women students of the time, all was not bad, because Hamilton was also trying to improve the social environment on campus and the safety and comfort in which female students lived. Prior to that time, almost all students had occupied private residences in Bozeman that provided room and board. In 1910, Hamilton Hall, dedicated to the president's deceased wife, was built to house the majority of female students. It marked the coming of age of Montana State as a full coeducational college.

In 1911 and 1912, the idea of Greek fraternity living was starting to emerge at MSC. In response to the construction of campus residences for women, a few male students organized the first two fraternities on campus.

But by 1913, they were not faring well. Pressure on them came from faculty members and President Hamilton himself, and the board of education insisted that the fraternities be banned because of concern that they were too exclusive. The ban itself discriminated. It was imposed on the college but not on Missoula's university campus. For a period of three years, MSC fraternities were reduced to the status of clubs, although they still operated along fraternity lines. The ban was lifted in 1916 in order to ease the burden placed on the dormitories and the boardinghouses in Bozeman caused by a surge in the number of students enrolled.[29]

In the late 1910s, the college started showing signs of growth, with the students becoming strongly patriotic and intensely proud of their institution. In 1916, a large group of college men climbed the bare face of a mountain north of Bozeman and constructed, out of rocks, a huge block letter M that was celebrated every fall. The new activity was perhaps a little too much for President Hamilton. By 1919, he had become tired of building the college and fighting with the University in Missoula. He wanted a quieter life and stepped down to the position of the dean of men, relinquishing the presidency to agronomist Alfred Atkinson.[30]

Back in 1914, there had been a vacancy for the head coaching job at Montana State College, and Hamilton seized upon it as an opportunity to lure Fred Bennion to the campus from Utah to take the job. Bennion was then thirty-one and had already become a legend in Utah coaching circles, having served as basketball coach at BYU (1908–10) and then as head football and basketball coach at the University of Utah (1910–14). Just before the start of football in the fall of 1914, Bennion said goodbye to the state of Utah and headed to Bozeman.[31]

What brought Fred Bennion to Montana State was not just the attraction of the coaching job. It was due in large part to a period of dire family circumstances. Tragedy had hit them earlier in the year, when both his father-in-law and brother-in-law were dying, leaving what was described as a "vast ranch and various other properties in Utah" without management.[32] To keep their family ranch alive, Fred had to give up his coaching job at Utah. By the end of the summer, the family crisis was over and he was free to return to coaching. By that time, however, it was not the only thing he wanted. He had started looking north toward Montana, because he had become interested in its vast agricultural lands and in the related agriculture courses at Montana State College. When Hamilton contacted Bennion about the Bobcat coaching vacancy, he jumped at the opportunity, and President Hamilton hired him.

Montana State would get more than just Fred Bennion. He had convinced Ott Romney to come with him to MSC as an assistant coach. But then Bennion had a better idea. Ott had one year of eligibility left, but under Rocky Mountain Conference rules, he was no longer eligible to compete for Utah. Montana State was not in the conference at the time, and its rules didn't apply. Maybe, just maybe, Ott could be a player. The idea stayed with Bennion, and it was only a short time before he put the question to Hamilton. After thinking about it, Hamilton got back and gave his approval. Ott Romney could work toward a master's degree in agriculture and play one year for the Bobcats.

Word had also reached Romney that President Hamilton was involved with the area's Rhodes scholarship committee and was anxious to get a young man of Ott's qualities on campus so he could nominate him. The scholarship didn't pan out for Ott, but the rest of the package did. Soon after he stepped on the playing field, it became apparent that Ott was one of the best all-around athletes to have attended the college. After starring for the Bobcats at quarterback during the football season, he easily transitioned to the starting five in basketball, playing both guard and forward. His knowledge of the game showed, and he was quickly being called one of the "headiest" players on the team.[33]

While the Bozeman boosters rejoiced at Ott's arrival, the University of Utah sports fans in Salt Lake City were resentful. Ott was back playing football and basketball again, but this time it was for Montana State College and not for them. BYU administrators and fans were also upset by the Utah star going to Bozeman, which added to the existing bad blood that caused the press to report that their BYU teams "did not receive a first-class reception in Montana, which accounts for their losing a couple of games."[34]

The unhappiness in Utah finally boiled over into a full-scale protest against Romney playing for the Bobcats. The people in Utah were claiming that he was now a professional and was being paid to play by MSC. Hamilton responded by saying that Romney was not receiving any money on account of athletics and that he was helping to earn his expenses by working in the "press bureau service." Bennion felt it was necessary to point out that Romney was there for studies and "the academic and eligibility standards of the College were as high as any Rocky Mountain Conference school."[35]

It wasn't just Utah and BYU that were agitating. The whole brouhaha of Romney being paid to play had first been stirred up by Utah State University's coach, C.T. Teetzel, in advance of the Bobcat's football game against the Aggies in Logan. The game was scheduled for October 17, 1914, and Teetzell wanted to keep Romney out of the contest. Looking for some responsible governing body to complain to, Teetzel was only able to find the Intermountain Association of the Amateur Athletic Union (AAU). He sought a gratuitous opinion from them that he hoped would give him a basis to delay the game; but that group had no control whatsoever over college athletics, and there was no investigation, so the game went ahead. The *Salt Lake Telegram* reported, "the 'cocky' Utah State team were handed the surprise party of their lives." In epic fashion, Ott Romney sought revenge against Teetzel and ran the football down his team's throat. Like a raging bull, he could not be stopped, and the Bobcats brutally punished the Aggies, 53–3. The whining Teetzel was soon fired.[36]

The Romney controversy did not go unnoticed by the in-state university in Missoula, which joined the angry voices from Utah, Utah State and BYU in complaints that Montana State was "hiring players." At the end of his second and last year at MSC, when he did not play football or basketball, the versatile Ott Romney was listed in the 1916 *Montanan* yearbook as both a graduate student in agriculture and an instructor in English. However, Ott had not enrolled in courses leading to a graduate degree. Instead, in 1916,

New gymnasium on the Montana State campus, 1923. *Montana State University*.

at the end of two years as a full-time student, he was awarded a bachelor's degree in agronomy.[37]

When the 1915 basketball season had started, Ott experienced a letdown. MSC's home games were played in a sparse, 1896 frame building called the Drill Hall. It originally had a dirt floor and no heat. A wood floor had recently been put in, as well as some wood-burning stoves, but there were only four rows of seats, and the low ceiling made it impossible to shoot high, arching shots.[38] Ott could not help making a mental comparison with Salt Lake City's elegant Deseret Gym, where large crowds had cheered him on when he played for Utah. "If only MSC had such a facility," he would say to himself. It was coming, but it was still a long way off.

4

ONWARD TO BILLINGS

Ott Romney Becomes a Coach

Mr. Romney holds A.B. and M.A. degrees from the University of Utah and a bachelor of science and agriculture degree from the Montana state college at Bozeman. In his college days, Mr. Romney starred in practically every form of sports and has an enviable collection of cups, medals and ribbons won in competition with the best teams in the mountain states section.
—Billings (MT) Gazette, *September 6, 1916*

In the spring of 1916, Ott Romney was considering his next move. He would have a degree in agriculture now to go with his other credentials, and he looked favorably at staying in Montana. There was something about it he liked, and certainly the agricultural community was expanding and playing an important patriotic part in sending food to Europe, which was engulfed in the Great War.

Agriculture became one option for him, and soon he added to that the possibility of getting a high school coaching job. He thought he knew where both his coaching abilities and his degree in agronomy might be put to use, and he headed for Billings, Montana.[39]

The head-coaching job at Billings High School was open, and he was hired to fill the vacancy. He moved into a sparse single room at the YMCA and also registered for the draft. His draft registration card said that he was twenty-four years old and was a teacher at Billings High School.[40] Based on his degree from Montana State, Romney was also hired to superintend the work of home gardening in Billings and boost conservation of the food supply. He was successful when $65,000 of vegetables were grown in his Billings gardens, and he encouraged the boys of the town to start growing produce. His program received awards for maintaining the gardens in approved fashion throughout the growing season.[41] In Billings, Ott Romney became influential, and he cut quite a figure. He was single and eligible, and the young ladies couldn't keep from talking about him and how fine he looked in his fashionable clothes.

Soon after he got to Billings High, in the fall of 1916, Ott had what may have been one of his worst ideas. Lonesome for his Salt Lake City family and friends and eager to display what he thought was his coaching prowess, he invited the Salt Lake City East High football team to come by train all the way up to Montana and play his Billings team on Thanksgiving Day. It was a disaster. His old high school won the game, 53–0, based on blinding speed and quickness that the Billings boys could not match. Worse yet, Fred Bennion was the referee and witnessed the slaughter up close and personal. Even still worse, the name Romney appeared on the roster as the quarterback of the Utah team. There was no humiliation worse than a family embarrassment.[42]

Things got even more punishing in basketball season, when Ott had to fulfill his part of the arrangement to exchange home games by taking his team on the train to Utah to play a three-game series against East High School in Deseret Gym. He had great faith and believed his Billings High team would make a good showing, but they were not up to the level of competition they faced. On the night of January 29, the East High Leopards doubly embarrassed Romney. First, the Billings boys, who were called "Kyotes," were mistakenly called the "Tigers" by the press for their orange and black colors; second, they were beaten by a score of 56–19. The *Salt Lake City Tribune* tried to avoid appearing to be obviously rubbing it in when it lauded the passing and floor work of the Montanans while criticizing their shooting. Better things had to come, but the next night it was much the same, with the Billings squad losing, 57–28. The next morning came the headline: "Romney's Crew of Hoop Men Does Not Show Class in Battle." It was the ultimate insult and personal embarrassment. For Ott and his defeated team, the low point of the second evening was the arranged postgame social meeting of the two teams for dinner at the Newhouse Hotel on Main Street—like the wolves dining with the lambs. Then the players had to uncomfortably attend a play together at the Wilkes Theater.[43] A third game was played, and Billings again lost badly. A dejected Ott Romney and his despondent team, heads bowed and saying little, climbed aboard their train for the gloomy ride back to Billings. To Ott, it was a lesson in humility and served as a painful motivator to make himself and his future teams better. He had come to realize that it took more than good coaching to win. It also took superior athletes—those who had speed, quickness, strength, coordination and stamina, as well as the size to match opponents. He vowed to develop these players, and he realized he would have to be very particular in picking them in the future.

5
THE GREAT WAR

Four Athletic Brothers of the Romney Family in the Service
—*Headline,* Salt Lake Telegram, *August 13, 1918*

In 1916 and 1917, with the United States called upon to provide manufactured goods and food for the war in Europe, the economy flourished in Montana. The Anaconda Copper Mining Company in Butte provided needed copper metal, and the broad plains of Montana provided wheat. When the United States finally entered the war in 1917, it did not take long before Montanans were enlisting. Others were drafted, and high quotas were set. When the Spanish flu pandemic swept around the world, many American troops waiting to be shipped overseas to the European front died in encampments on American soil.[44] Shortly after, in 1918, the Great War was over.

In the meantime, when the war effort in the country reached a high pitch, posters appeared everywhere urging enlistment, and Ott Romney in Billings and his brothers in Utah would be looking at a scowling Uncle Sam, pointing a long finger and reading, "I Want You in the Army." Ott Romney had not been called to duty right away, and he continued his coaching duties at Billings High School. On March 4, 1918, he enlisted in the U.S. Naval Reserves, to be trained in flying. Three of his brothers in Utah enlisted at the same time, giving the family four members in the military, something the Salt Lake City newspaper picked up on and reported.[45]

Finally, in April, Ott received his orders to report, and a big sendoff banquet was arranged for him at the Northern Hotel in Billings, with friends, family and about fifty students attending.[46] A pretty girl, Ruth Harding, an eighteen-year-old college freshman from MSC, was also there. She had graduated from Billings High School the previous year. It was apparent that she and Ott had a mutual attraction.

With good wishes from all, Ott went off to a flying school to prepare for war, but his service time soon ended when the pandemic swept around the globe. He was released as a lieutenant on November 25, 1918, in plenty of time to get home for Christmas. The fighting had come to an end on November 11, 1918, following an armistice between the Allies and Germany that called for a cease-fire effective at 11:00 a.m.—the eleventh hour of the eleventh day of the eleventh month. Ott's family and many fans were glad to celebrate it and welcome back the Utah sports hero.[47]

Arriving home, Ott was seen strolling the wide streets of Salt Lake City and receiving the welcoming smiles of his townspeople. But before he settled in, he had an important involvement in Montana, and he was soon off to Billings again. This time, he had only one thing in mind, and that was to see Ruth Harding. When Ott proposed marriage, she accepted.

Ruth's decision was not popular with her father, because she had dropped out of college at Montana State—and he didn't like Ott. He vowed not to attend the wedding. Despite what might have been said to her, she was of legal age to make her own decisions, and she and Ott got their marriage license on March 3. Ruth turned nineteen on March 6, 1919, the day of the wedding. Only her mother attended. There was no one around to provide an LDS ceremony, so a Congregational minister in Livingston married them at 9:00 a.m.[48] The newlyweds stayed in Montana just long enough to say goodbye and then left for Salt Lake City, where Ott took on his new coaching duties at East High School. Utah had finally gotten him back.[49]

As coach at East High, one of Ott Romney's goals was to get the players in the best physical condition possible. They had talent, but as a group, they needed to improve with a stronger training regimen. This would prove frustrating. When Ott undertook the task of running the training workouts himself, he soon found he did not have the time required to work individually with each player. He looked for an assistant, only to find that his budget did not provide for the position.

One day during practice, Romney observed a janitor leaning on his broom and intently watching the practice. The man seemed interested in what was going on. The next day, he was back again. Over several days, Ott saw him enough times that he became curious and went over to talk. Ott found out that the man's name was Schubert Dyche, and much to Ott's surprise, he discovered that the janitor had a significant athletic background and was interested in the dynamism Romney displayed to inspire the players to put out their best efforts.

Ott could see that "Schube," as he was often called, was a strong, wiry five-foot, nine-inch athlete, appearing to be in tip-top shape from his own conditioning exercises, which included running and lifting. Dyche could be seen in the high school gym working out after his custodial duties were completed.[50] Soon, Ott and Schube were talking regularly at all the practices, and Dyche was given a chance to help after practice by running the team's conditioning and weight-training drills. As a few weeks went by, Romney found some money in the budget to pay Dyche as his assistant. Although the wages weren't good, Dyche took the job to heart and spent long hours with the coach and the players in their pursuit of wins against stiff competition in the sports mecca of Salt Lake City. This was enough to elevate the janitor to a new position as an instructor in physical education and hygiene, but he could still be seen pushing his broom. It was necessary to give him additional income to support his musical pursuits, which he hoped would find him a regular spot in an orchestra. If that wasn't enough diversity of interests, Dyche's analytical mind also gave him a passion for word games; he once finished sixteenth in a national crossword puzzle contest.[51]

Ott Romney believed that coaching should teach techniques that would fix a player's responses in a game, without delay of thought. He wanted his players to be spontaneous, but first he had to pay attention to their individual habits. Practices were a mixture of individual drills and teamwork. Ott also believed that as a first order, a successful coach had to be good at public relations. On this point he and the taciturn Schubert were different. Ott also believed that coaches had to be intelligent individuals; it was Dyche's intelligence that drew Romney to him.[52] What was more, the players were loyal to Dyche.

Schubert's genuine dedication to sports and physical fitness infected the players he trained. His sparse praise was enough

Schubert Dyche. *Montana State College 1928 Yearbook.*

to inspire them. He and Romney had formed an unwritten and unspoken partnership that in the end would result in a national championship basketball team at Montana State College in 1929. But by then Romney was no longer the head coach—Schubert Dyche, the former janitor at Salt Lake's East High School, was.

6

MSC GETS A NEW PRESIDENT AND A NEW GYM

We have come a long way from the three "R"s….We have substituted them with the three "H"s—the head, the heart and the hand—with a rather marked emphasis on the hand.
—*Alfred Atkinson*[53]

Bozeman had grown since the turn of the century, when MSC was just starting. Gone now in downtown were the dirt streets of the late 1800s and the brothels and old saloons frequented by wagon men and soldiers from nearby pioneer Fort Ellis. They had been replaced by a few stately houses on Willson Avenue. Schools, churches and well-established businesses were starting to emerge, along with the flourishing of the medical profession and the building of a hospital. A tradition of fine buildings had started back in 1903, when the Bozeman Carnegie Library was built in a classical revival style with Doric columns supporting a triangular pediment at the entrance. Some said it was intentionally placed across the street from the red-light district and opium dens of the old downtown. It represented a departure from the past and a step into the future. At the center of Bozeman's progress was the college, where top-notch education was starting to flourish. Now, at the start of the 1920s, the Montana State administrators were having visions of a campus featuring buildings that were not just functional but also designed in the classic academic architectural styles of the times.

In 1919, when agronomist Alfred Atkinson was inaugurated as college president, he told those assembled: "We have come a long way from the three 'R's.…We have substituted them with the three 'H's—the head, the heart and the hand—with a rather marked emphasis on the hand." The emphasis under the new president would be on agriculture, engineering and the domestic sciences, all leading to usefulness in hands-on professions. In 1920, the college was given a new name to highlight the curricula: Montana State College of Agriculture and Mechanical Arts (MSC). The academic buildings that would soon be constructed in the 1920s would reflect this emphasis.[54]

In the cold winter months of the 1921–22 school year, MSC president Alfred Atkinson often walked out of his office on the fourth floor of tall Montana Hall and across the hallway's squeaking floor to look out the large windows to the south. He could see a number of busy construction sites. There were five magnificent buildings going up simultaneously on campus, thanks to a generous bond issue passed by Montana voters in the 1920 election.[55,56] The project that intrigued Atkinson the most was relatively close, and even in the snow-covered winter landscape, the massive new gymnasium was impressively rising, thanks to the efforts of nearly one hundred chilled workmen, who were glad to have the employment despite the weather.

Atkinson first saw the concrete foundation being poured, and then, as the weeks went by, the gym building rose above the concrete. The steel framework was put in place; then, one brick at a time, the masons laid the base for the walls. Inside the perimeter was a sub-basement, illuminated by large, natural light–shedding windows placed high on the walls. Atkinson was dedicating this space for incoming freshman to be taught physical education, as well as for gymnastics and volleyball. It was also to be an indoor exercise area where students and players on the Bobcat teams could stay in condition. Along the south wall of the building were four recessed handball courts in the basement. An indoor swimming pool was being installed on the second floor. On the third floor was the basketball court.

The imposing structure's exterior was finished with red-and-green-colored bricks and a reddish-brown terra-cotta cladding. Architect George H. Shanley from Great Falls, a flourishing town on the Missouri River about two hundred miles north of Bozeman, had been awarded the contract to design the building to be at a construction cost of $225,000. It was the second-most expensive of the five new buildings going up, exceeded only by the new engineering building ($250,000).[57,58]

In 1922, Atkinson and a cohort of his faculty sat down to design a promotional flyer for the college. Shown were all the new campus buildings and their accompanying names: Hamilton Hall, Roberts Hall, Ryan Lab,

1929 Basketball National Champions

Montana State College's new gym under construction in 1922. *Montana State University*.

Lewis Hall, Montana Hall and Traphagen Hall. But no name had been given to the new gym; it would be known for years simply as the MSC Gymnasium. Despite the building being nameless, what most pleased Atkinson was the elegant home it provided for his basketball team. As a newer member of the respected Rocky Mountain Conference (its official name was the Rocky Mountain Faculty Athletic Conference), MSC would never again have to be embarrassed by playing in the dilapidated Drill Hall. The new gym also brought with it bragging rights—significant in Utah. Its footprint bested the Deseret Gym in Salt Lake City by just over 100 square feet; the MSC gym measured 163 by 99 feet, compared to the Deseret Gym at 150 by 90 feet.

Along with the new buildings on campus came additional science laboratories and engineering experiment space. Atkinson was comfortable in saying that his college was now truly ready to take its place as the "MIT of the West." It was something both he and his predecessor, Hamilton, had envisioned.[59] Not publicized as much was the full campus life that Atkinson looked for as part of an outstanding school. It included watching great athletic teams competing against top-notch regional and national competition. This was a big boast for a small school huddled in a far northern valley in the Rocky Mountains with only 750 students.[60][61]

The college in Bozeman had never had an exclusive claim to the name Montana State. Over the mountains to the west some two hundred miles

Drill Hall at Montana State College. *Montana State University*.

Drill Hall basketball court. *Montana State University*.

was Montana State University in Missoula. It wasn't until 1965 that its name became the University of Montana, at the same time that Montana State College became Montana State University, with the obvious confusion. The two institutions had always been different. In Missoula, students and faculty of the liberal arts institution would lord it over their counterparts at Montana State College, calling it the "cow college." The university in turn earned the rejoinder that it was a "dancing school." Over the years, the battles between the college Bobcats and the university Grizzlies became epic.

7

SCHUBERT REILLY DYCHE

Schubert Dyche has the edge on other mountain football coaches in one respect, at least....Anytime he's feeling low, he can seek success on the piccolo, flute or cello....He's accomplished with all three and one year toured the state with the Montana Symphony orchestra.
—Greeley (CO) Daily Tribune, *1942*[62]

Another man from East High School in Salt Lake City eventually made it to Montana State College. He was Schubert Reilly Dyche, the former janitor who had become Ott Romney's assistant. He was a person of contradictions, a result of his native intelligence conflicting with the hard molding of the uncertain times on the Great Plains when he was growing up.[63]

Dyche was born in 1893 in Kansas into a family of farmers. His kinfolk had been there since his grandfather left West Virginia and came west with the hard-stock settlers who had worked their way across the country. The family lived in the small community of Wakarusa, Shawnee County, just seven miles from Topeka, where Schubert was born. His first contradiction came at birth, when he was given the name Schubert, after Austrian composer Franz Schubert. His mother, Eliza Conron, had a love for music, and Schubert's Ave Maria had been played at her wedding to Edward Alexander Dyche on March 22, 1892, at her parent's farm home in Wakarusa.[64] After the wedding, the young couple boarded the Atchison, Topeka and Santa Fe Railway train no. 113 bound for New Mexico, where they planned to reside on a ranch. But they were soon back in Wakarusa, running a grocery store and planning a family. Baby Schubert was their first child.[65]

Schubert Dyche learned as a young boy that his family had curiosity about many things. His uncle Lewis Dyche had not gone to school until he was fifteen but somehow worked his way through college and became a professor of zoology at Kansas University in Lawrence. He became known as an excellent taxidermist and mounted the remains of the horse Comanche found on the Little Big Horn battlefield after the 1876 defeat there of George Armstrong Custer's Seventh Cavalry.[66][67]

Schubert was often told that he should follow in his uncle's footsteps if he didn't want to be tied down to a family grocery store. In Wakarusa, his father's store had operated successfully until his eye coveted a bigger market; in 1906, he and the family moved to Topeka to open the Green Front Grocery. Schubert, thirteen years old, was already conscripted to stock shelves and clean up after hours. All appeared well for a time until, one morning, the *Topeka Daily Capital* reported the shocking news that Edward Dyche had vanished! He had left a key where his wholesale supplier could find it, and the newspaper could only speculate that he had used credit heavily and couldn't pay off his bills and that this was the cause for his swift departure. A devastated Eliza Dyche told customers and friends that she did not know where Edward was but expected to hear from him soon.[68]

That about did it for Schubert Dyche's family in Kansas. Their reputation had been ruined. When Edward finally showed up, he and Eliza thought it best to move on to greener pastures. They went first to Boulder, Colorado, where Edward continued in the grocery business. But things were tough there, so they moved to Pueblo, Colorado, then the largest steel-manufacturing town west of the Mississippi. Edward was unaccountably unemployed for twenty-four months before he got on as a laborer in a steel mill with the giant Colorado Fuel and Iron Company (CF&I). The company also owned its own local railroad to haul supplies, ore and finished products. It was a large business enterprise, and from 1901 to 1912, CF&I's common stock was known by investors to be one of the Dow Industrials.[69][70]

By the time the Dyche family got to Pueblo, they had added six more children, and as though that wasn't enough for the careworn parents, they also took in Edward's aging father, Alexander.[71] Soon, another son was born. In the large, struggling family, much was demanded of its eldest son, and Schubert's life was full of chores, weekend work and care of his younger siblings. It was a deadly serious existence, and Schubert grew up to be a deadly serious man. No time was to be wasted on frivolity, and the family's reputation had to be built on an uncompromising work ethic. Even in his early academic life, Schubert would not avoid hard tasks, and when he went to high school, his coursework included units in Latin and algebra.[72] Schubert knew from an early age that he had to perform, and perform well. He was his own harshest critic.[73] With his natural athletic abilities and the continuous hard labor he performed even while going to school, he grew up strong and competitive. As a boy, he excelled in sports.

Strangely, it wasn't just sports Schubert was determined to master. Motivated by his mother's desire to have him trained on an instrument, he learned clarinet at an early age, then the flute and finally the oboe, becoming proficient in all three. Along the way, he also added the cello. He came to love the discipline of musicians and the intensity of their performances and played wherever and whenever he could in orchestras and bands.

When his high school days were over, Schubert moved on to the University of Colorado in Boulder, where the family had once lived and where he could stay with friends. In three years there, he excelled in athletics, particularly baseball, and he had all As and Bs as a math and physics major. He easily earned credits as well in Shakespearean language and the history of philosophy. Schubert was twenty-one when he had to drop out of college and move back to Pueblo to help his family and work at the steel company as a laborer. He toiled hard to improve his image and advanced to a job checking the safety and performance of the company's railway cars, where he had the title of car inspector.[74] [75]

In 1917, as a twenty-four-year-old single man, Schubert reported for the draft. His registration card said he was tall, slender, had gray eyes and brown hair and had been a college student for three years. When he was drafted and sent overseas, he did not go to the front as a soldier. Rather, the army took notice of his musical talents and assigned him the classification and rank of musician first class and sent him to join a military band in France, at La Rochelle. Soon after, Schubert was shipped back to the United States aboard the steamship *Mongolia*, which docked in New Jersey on May 9, 1918. From there, he took trains home to join his parents.[76] [77]

Upon his return, Schubert soon learned that Coloradoans were basking in the success of a native son, boxer Jack Dempsey of Manassa, a town close to Pueblo. On December 19, 1919, in Toledo, Ohio, Dempsey defeated Jess Willard for the World Heavyweight Boxing Championship. Afterward, he became known worldwide as the "Manassa Mauler." Dempsey's success showed Schubert and other local athletes that anything was possible, no matter where they were from, and it instilled in them the goals and the work ethic required to make them excel in their athletic endeavors.[78]

In 1919, with the war over and his family stabilized for once, Schubert, now twenty-six, returned to the University of Colorado. They were looking for a baseball coach, and he could almost fill the bill. He had the skills and some experience, but he did not have a college degree, which the university required. It appeared that the solution was to enroll him in school and put him on the team, listed as a new player. Observers would note, however, that he was not attired as a regular player. Instead, he had a jacket over his uniform, arms folded and scowling. It may have been that he was actually serving as the coach of the team.[79]

By 1920, Schubert's father had performed well enough in the railway operations of CF&I to embolden him to move to the west slope of the Rocky Mountains in hopes of landing a better railway job in Utah.[80] Abandoning his attempts to get a degree at Colorado, Schubert moved to join the family at their new address on North Main Street in Salt Lake City. It was just up the hill above the magnificent Mormon Temple, which the family admired. But they were not Latter-day Saints, nor did they have much interest in other churches. What Edward Dyche did find in Utah was the new employment he was looking for, with the Denver and Rio Grande Western Railway, where he remained as a clerk until his passing in 1939.[81]

Still trying to use his talents, Schubert turned to music in a town where it was a tradition, led by the LDS Church with its already famous choir performing just a few blocks away in the acoustically perfect Tabernacle in Temple Square. He joined with the Willard Weihe string quartet and renowned pianist Ruth Williams. In one performance, Schubert played two flute solos: one, the obscure "The Sweet of the Year" by Mary Turner Salter; the other, the difficult "Charming Bird" overture from *La Perle Du Brésil* by F. David.[82] Despite his notable appearances, his engagements with orchestral groups around town paid only a small amount in honorariums and did not bring in enough income to live on.

Impressed as he was by the Tabernacle as a music venue, Schubert was even more inspired by the nearby Deseret Gym as a sports venue. It stood just east of Temple Square and had a fitness room, a swimming pool and a running track, all of which he used regularly. The huge three-story building also housed a large basketball court, where Schubert would see the University of Utah Utes play.[83] It fascinated him.

While Schubert Dyche was at East High, he made the most of his free time in the summers. He knew that someday he wanted to be a head coach,

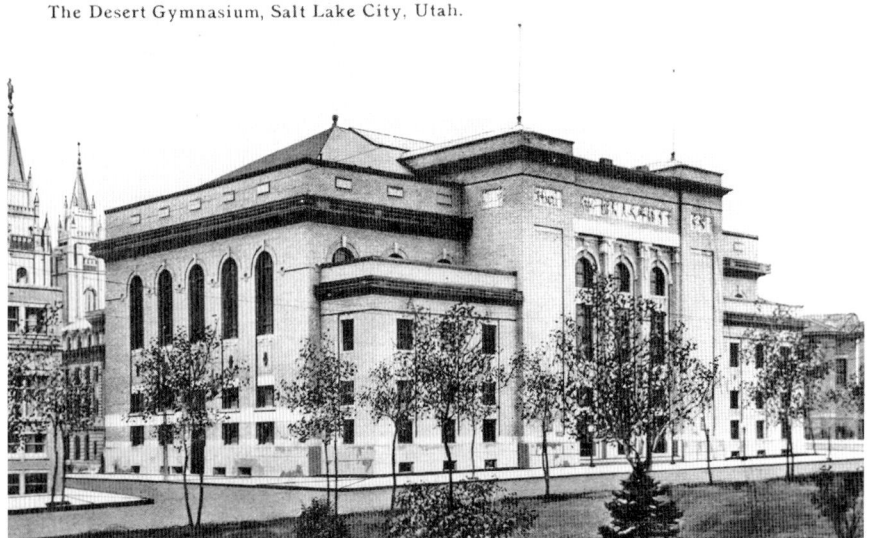

The Desert Gymnasium, Salt Lake City, Utah.

Deseret Gym in Salt Lake City. *Courtesy University of Utah Photo Archives or Utah State Historical Society.*

something for which he needed to complete a college degree. He was smart, and he wanted a good education, so he took summer school classes at the University of California–Berkeley and at Stanford University at Palo Alto, where he received training in physical education under recognized visiting professors from Pennsylvania and Chicago. He got the college work there he was looking for, but he still needed more credits to graduate.[84]

Shubert wanted to help other people. In 1922, he took a job summer job at Fort Bayard, New Mexico, in a tuberculosis sanatorium. He had compassion for the people there and found he could help them. He also played baseball there. As ideal as his life was, at the end of the summer, he went back to Salt Lake City to resume his duties under Romney.[85] He was also hoping to find a way in some capacity to start working his way into the organized sports of the Rocky Mountain Conference. His first step was to apply to be an approved football referee, which was granted at the conference meeting in March 1923.[86]

8

THE DEVELOPMENT OF BASKETBALL IN THE UNITED STATES

On account of the proximity of the players of this game to the spectators, it takes on a special form of attraction. The weather never causes a postponement, and the spectators have the comforts of the indoors. These phases of the game along with others have brought it to a state of poularity that has surpassed the originator's fondest dreams.
—Forrest C. "Phog" Allen from his 1924 book My Basketball Bible[87]

The sport of basketball, which so enamored Ott Romney and Schubert Dyche, would not have existed had it not been for the cold winter months of 1891 at Springfield College in Massachusetts. It was there that Dr. James Naismith was tasked with coming up with a new game to be played indoors. He did it by hanging peach baskets up high for teams to throw soccer balls into. Soon, the baskets were replaced with steel rims and netting. In 1894, Naismith was unhappy with the size of the soccer ball, so he asked a meatpacking company in New York that also dealt in animal by-products to construct a larger, heavier ball.[88] Eventually, that company, Schwarzschild & Sulzberger (later to be Sulzberger & Sons), founded Ashland Manufacturing Company to make balls, tennis racket strings, violin strings and surgical sutures. It soon expanded into baseball shoes and tennis racquets.[89] In time, the company became Wilson Sporting Goods.

The early basketballs were made from sheets of tanned leather glued to canvas, from which panels were cut, to be sewn together to form a sphere. There was an opening between two of the panels to insert a rubber bladder with an air tube sticking out. When the ball was inflated, heavy rawhide laces

Montana State's Golden Bobcats

James Naismith. *Courtesy Naismith National Basketball Hall of Fame.*

closed the opening over the tube, leaving a protrusion on the surface that would make the ball almost impossible to dribble. Advances were made in the 1920s, and by 1927, basketballs appeared with a pair of abutting leather flaps covering the laces to leave a smoother surface.[90] The newer balls made dribbling an exciting feature of the game, and the dribblers started having a field day, bulling their way through defenses while bouncing the ball. To put a check on them, the rules committee decided that a dribbler who simply barged into a defender would be called for a foul, called "charging." Basketball was becoming modernized, and it was all to the benefit of teams like the Montana State Bobcats under Ott Romney, which had quick, agile players, the personification of which was Cat Thompson.[91] [92] [93]

In those days, there were no national championship tournaments; instead, teams were encouraged to seek out the best games they could find that would showcase their talented players to the fans in, and beyond, their region. In Montana State's case, the region was vast. Travel by visiting teams to Bozeman, or by the Bobcats to the home courts of many of the other good teams, could take days on uncomfortable railway passenger trains steaming over uneven tracks. This was not necessarily the case on the crowded East Coast or in the populated Midwest, where getting to and from games was easier.

9

OTT ROMNEY'S EARLY YEARS AS MONTANA STATE'S COACH

For the Bobcat Spirit is a big spirit, like the big distances of the country in which it thrives: and it is a splendid, fiery spirit, like the sunsets which light the western skies. It is a spirit of rugged endurance like the mountains which inspire it, and a spirit of unselfishness like the mood of Nature when she blessed the West.
—*Ott Romney, "The Bobcat Spirit," 1923* Montanan[94]

On Sunday, July 2, 1922, sports fans in Salt Lake City awoke to a disheartening headline in the *Salt Lake Tribune*: "Leopards Lose Famous Coach. Ott Romney Goes to Bozeman." The writer lamented that an "attractive offer" had lured Ott and that he would report as head coach for the Montana State College teams in September. It was noted that Romney "was almost idolized by the students and faculty and he was…regarded as a wizard in athletic work." One other person, who would become important sometime later at Montana State, was mentioned. The article said that Romney had "built from a one-man system to a staff of five men," one of whom was "Schubert Dyche, third team coach and instructor in physical education." For the time being, Dyche had to be left behind in Utah.

Ott was immediately confronted with a clamor of disappointment and disbelief from astonished friends and boosters at East High School and the University of Utah. "Don't go," they implored. They told him that if he stayed, he could replace retiring head coach Tommy Fitzpatrick with the Utes. Now that they were about to lose him, there was a newly created awareness in Utah that he was considered college head-coaching material and should stay in the Salt Lake Valley, or at least in Utah. However, the deal was done, and Ott saw his best opportunity in Montana, where he also had fans and supporters from his time as a player at Montana State and as a coach at Billings High School. Besides, the brand-new gymnasium on campus was crying for a championship team. With a sad farewell to fans and well-wishers, he and Ruth got into their car and started the long drive north over the mountains on the dirt roads to Montana.[95]

When they reached the Gallatin Valley, Ott Romney was once again impressed with its beauty, just as he had been when he arrived there in 1914 as a player. Once in Bozeman, he got right down to business, welcoming the football team to its first practice, only to be disappointed with the players who met him that day. To him, they seemed out of shape and lacking in school spirit, which he vowed to instill in them. His encouragement worked, and by the time basketball season rolled around, Ott's teams were an immediate success. His 1922–23 team went 18-3, and his 1923–24 team was even better, at 20-3.[96]

There had always been a nagging doubt in the minds of college basketball coaches and boosters in the lightly settled Mountain West that their teams could measure up to the quality of play at the older and larger universities in the more populated areas to the east and on the Pacific coast. In reality, that question had been answered in 1917, when the whole world learned that Washington State College, in the remoteness of eastern Washington State in the railway hub town of Pullman, had an astounding 25-1 record. Playing against stiff competition on the Pacific coast, the team's only loss was a 28–20 game against California in Berkeley. That year, the Washington State Cougars were the consensus national champions and later received that same crown from the Helms Foundation of Los Angeles, at the time the foremost authority in ranking college basketball teams. Helms was later acknowledged by almost everyone to be the authority on national college basketball champions for the first half of the twentieth century.[97]

Back in 1917, when Ott Romney read the newspaper story about Washington State's championship, he had become convinced that the only real barriers to a western team winning the championship were in the mind. He saw the possibility of such a heroic feat being repeated, even for a small remote college like Montana State. There were two conditions. First, they would have to recruit the best players available in the region. Second, the college would have to have finances to commit to good facilities and cover the expenses of railway transportation for the long trips that were required to play at the larger schools. He had other thoughts, but those he had to file away in his mind, because it would be another five years before he became a head coach. Luckily, he would land the job at MSC in Bozeman.

When he did get to Montana State in 1922 as coach, he couldn't help comparing its new gymnasium with Salt Lake's Deseret Gym. He started to see that basketball would be important here; his future might not be that bad in this small mountain town, even though it was far from the premier college basketball teams in the country. Most of them were clustered in the Atlantic, Midwest and Southwest states. The state of Kansas had great success with basketball, and it was there that the immortal coach Phog Allen was revolutionizing the sport. Looking back in history, Yale had been the first national champion, in 1901, and again in 1903, separated by Minnesota in 1902, which repeated in 1917. Then it was Columbia for two years in 1904 and 1905, followed by Dartmouth the next year. In 1907, Chicago, under its famous mentor, Amos Alonzo Stagg, started a three-year run as national champion, followed in 1910 by Columbia again, and then St. Johns in New York City, where the mammoth Madison Square Garden was seeing its first basketball games. Wisconsin won championships in 1912, 1914 and 1916, separated by Navy in 1913 and Illinois in 1915. Then there was the monumental break in the basketball hierarchical order when Washington State won its title.[98]

10
OTT ROMNEY BUILDS A TEAM AT MONTANA STATE

For when it comes to handling athletes, governing their training and getting the most out of them, Romney doesn't have to take a back seat for any of them in his class.
—Anaconda Standard, *July 6, 1922*

Eventually, Montana State College joined the Rocky Mountain Conference, where it would face stiff competition in its western division against Utah, Utah State and Brigham Young University. The school would have to get the best players it could. In the spring of 1923, Ott Romney could see that he had only one exceptional basketball player returning, and that was Adolph Hartwig, a tall sophomore center from Forsyth, Montana, who could run, score, pass the ball well and shoot from outside. Ott needed another big man and persuaded Valery "Val" Glynn, a player he had coached at East High in Salt Lake City, to come to Bozeman. Another new man had been recruited from his own family, when his brother agreed to come to MSC. Floyd Romney was an excellent athlete; the previous year, he had played for Utah as a fullback in football and as a forward in basketball.[99]

Even though Ott was happy to have Hartwig returning and the new players coming in, they had not been tested as a team, and he was not confident as to how they would perform in Montana State's first year in the Rocky Mountain Conference. He need not have been worried, because at the end of the season, it was reported that the 1923–24 Bobcats would "stand out in the history of the college…the Bobcats finished their 1924 hoop season in a blaze of glory." Of thirty-one games, the team won an amazing twenty-eight, with the Bobcats averaging almost 30 points a game while using a man-to-man defense that held opponents to about half that amount. Things were getting serious now, and Ott thought he had a good enough source of basketball talent to make good on the promise he had made to himself, to President Atkinson and to the loyal Bozeman boosters, to win the conference championship. It would be a daunting task, and he readied himself for both the praise and the criticism that would come.

After the end of his second season, in 1924, Romney went after Schubert Dyche, his former assistant at East High, and he succeeded in hiring him. He knew that the multitalented Dyche's eccentric personality might be viewed by some as a problem. Dyche was a man who could switch gears immediately. He could go from team practices to the orchestra, then to reading scientific articles and doing word puzzles at night, but Romney accepted him with his intellectual interests. What he really saw as Schubert's strong point was his insistence on physical conditioning, not only in his players but also in himself. He led by example, and the players followed him. Above all, Schube's intellect made him an ideal partner in strategizing games.[100]

In the fall of 1925, with the help of Schubert, Ott Romney started to look for ways to get this team more scoring opportunities. Offenses were usually slow, fixed and immobile, making it hard to get shots. Even with the shots they got, the team suffered criticism, and a cynical sports reporter from Bozeman had given his opinion on one of their early games. "It is the poorest shooting average that Montana State has made this season. The number of shots they had at the basket proves their eye trouble, as well as it proves their ability to work the ball into position for shooting against the best of teams."[101]

In those days, if a player was a forward, he was usually designated either right forward or left forward, and the guards either right guard or left guard. They did not switch sides of the court. Nor did the guards and forwards change positions when the team went from offense to defense. The teams typically moved as a unit up and down the court, rather than having the taller players under the basket on both offense and defense.

After talking it over with Schubert, Ott decided he had to take some of the rigidity out of the traditional offense if he was going to improve the shooting. When it came time to plan his starting lineup for the 1925–26 season, he took a bold step and put his center, Hartwig, up front at forward. Valery Glynn would be the center, and he was given some freedom of movement around the court. The problem was that it would leave the defensive basket more open than Ott would like, and that might be a disaster. He worried about what to do, but it would not be for long.

11

JOHN WILLIAM "BRICK" BREEDEN

The greatest mistake any student can make during his college career is to monopolize his time for studying. You may ask why I put activities first. The answer is, for no other reason than I consider activities the greatest thing in college.
—*Brick Breeden, president of Associated Students, 1929* Montanan

When basketball practice started in 1925, Romney and Dyche noticed that there was a new figure leaning on a broom in a dark corner of the Bobcat gymnasium. It was Jacob Breeden, a fifty-six-year-old janitor who was there to watch his gangling son start his career as a Bobcat. At the age of twenty-one, John William "Brick" Breeden was only a freshman and beginning his first college practice with the Montana State College basketball team.[102] At home, neither Jacob nor his wife, Flossie, called their son by his given name. No one did. In tribute to his sandy red hair, he was always called "Brick." The name stuck for the rest of his life, and soon the college basketball community, even far to the east, would know it.

The Breeden family had not been in Bozeman that long. Jacob was born in Roscoe, St. Clair County, Missouri, in 1869, and he lived there the next forty years, becoming a farmer and starting a family with six children. In 1919, things turned bad for Jacob and Flossie, as it had for many in the country, and they had to sell their property and board a steamboat bound upriver on the Missouri River to seek a better life in Montana. They settled on some land near the tiny town of Andes in northeastern Montana, but quite soon they could see that farming on a 360-acre homestead could barely feed the family, let alone produce a cash crop. They moved a short distance east to Fairview, Montana, where Jacob found work and a house to live in, but they soon discovered they were not in Montana at all, but instead across the state line dividing Montana from North Dakota that ran down the center of Fairview's Main Street. When the census taker came to their small home on January 24, 1920, the family included Jacob (fifty) and Flossie (forty-seven) and their seven children, of whom a nineteen-year-old daughter was the oldest. John William "Brick," at sixteen, was the second oldest.[103]

Jacob had little formal education to offer, although his intelligence was shown when, in Oyer, Missouri, he had quickly memorized enough Masonic lodge scripture to advance rapidly through the degrees of Masonry. Tired of the disappointment of farming, he set out to look for more permanent work. He had heard of Bozeman, Montana, and the campus at Montana State College, where the growth of the school and the addition of five new buildings, one of them a magnificent gymnasium, had created some jobs. Arriving in Bozeman, Jacob applied for a maintenance job at the college and was accepted as a custodian at a living wage. His family settled into Bozeman, moving eventually to a house in one of the newer residential areas close to the campus.[104]

By the time the Breedens got to Bozeman in 1921, Brick was seventeen years old, and because of his family's movements, he had not regularly attended school. He could do so now by enrolling as a freshman at Bozeman High School. He was well over six feet tall, and he immediately made an impact as a starting lineman on the football team, which needed all the help it could get. Despite the heroic efforts of his teammate Gus Wylie as a running quarterback, Brick's team lost to Great Falls High School, 62–0. It was a defeat that neither Brick nor Wylie would forget, or wish to repeat. After that, Brick's athletic life was in earnest, and losing was not acceptable.[105]

When Brick's first basketball season rolled around at Bozeman High, he approached it with an intensity that made him stand out right away. Because he had not played organized basketball until then, his size and athletic ability suited him best as a non-shooting guard defending under the opponent's basket. Later, as Brick developed his game, Coach Chauner of Bozeman thought a change to forward or center could be made. That never happened, because what Chauner saw during the year was a classic rim defender—a player with long arms and quick feet who could block shots, get in front of opponents, fill passing lanes and, above all, rebound. And it wasn't just getting the rebounds; it was also the outlet passes to get the ball downcourt to open teammates. Seldom did Brick score or even

Brick Breeden as a serious student in 1928. Montanan 1928, Montana State College Yearbook. *Montana State University*.

take shots. Other players could do that, and why squander his talent by taking him out of a defensive position that totally derailed the opponent's offense? After his first year in high school, no coach ever again wanted to move Brick from his defensive guard spot.

Soon enough, the honors came. In March, Brick Breeden was named to the official basketball all-state team as a guard. The best was yet to come. After Brick's final year for Bozeman High School on the basketball court, he was selected to the five-man all-time, all-state team in Montana, which spanned 1911 through 1925. Three of the players had competed prior to 1914; Brick and one excellent player, a boy named Frank Worden out of Butte, were from the current year.[106] And so Brick Breeden, having only somewhat recently arrived from Missouri, ended his high school basketball playing days as a celebrated Montana player.

Ott Romney had been interested in Breeden for his team. Ott could see Brick's incredible defensive abilities, and he had not overlooked his lack of any demonstrated scoring abilities. All the same, he wanted to give him a chance. At that time, Romney and other coaches were starting to give more attention to scoring, and the game was shifting to a philosophy of getting baskets on as many possessions as possible to outscore the other team, rather than playing a conservative game, with players staying back on defense. But why not have both, Ott reasoned. If a team could find a single great defender who would stay ready to go back while his team was on offense, then you could have it both ways, with the other four players fully attacking the basket. Although he would come in as a freshman, the maturity was there, as Brick was already twenty-one. Ott Romney's dream of a high-scoring offensive team was about to come true, by of all things recruiting a defensive giant who would free up the offense. Ott could hardly wait for Brick to enroll at MSC. Not only did Brick excel on the basketball court, but with his maturity, he also excelled in the classroom. Once he got to MSC, his activities were beyond just basketball, and in his senior year, his picture appeared in the college yearbook not only as captain of his team but also as president of the student body.[107]

12

THE 1925–26 BOBCATS

The Beginning of the Future

The trip was undoubtedly the most successful ever undertaken by any College team of the Northwest and the fine record and sportsmanship displayed by the Montana State College team insures this trip as an annual affair growing each year in length and quality of teams met.
—1926 Montanan

Once the basketball team had been assembled in the fall of 1925, Ott Romney could access the potential of the group, and he had a bold idea for their improvement. Gathering his thoughts and planning his words carefully, he walked out of the gym and across the campus to Montana Hall, where he climbed the two flights of creaking wooden stairs to President Alfred Atkinson's office. Being ushered in, he announced that he was there to talk about a new approach to basketball he wanted to use at MSC. Ott's plea was simple. He wanted to better prepare the team for the rigors of the Rocky Mountain Conference schedule, particularly against Utah, Utah State and Brigham Young Universities, each loaded with talent from the local basketball mecca. To do this, he proposed to Atkinson that the team take an extended trip during the Christmas break. They would play as many quality western teams as possible on their home courts—teams with more talent and skill than those from the smaller colleges in Montana that had always provided preseason warm-up games.

Sitting in his three-piece suit and with a quizzical look, Atkinson listened intently to Romney. The president was a hardworking, active leader, and his

Montana Hall at Montana State College. *Courtesy Library of Congress.*

ear was on the pulse of the community and the campus. He knew that some members of the faculty would always urge for the withdrawal of Montana State from the Rocky Mountain Conference to get rid of the distraction from rigorous academics. But to Atkinson, intercollegiate sports were important for any university or college. Montana State had to be in the regional Rocky Mountain Conference, and it had to perform well.

When Ott emerged from the meeting, there was a smile on his face. President Atkinson had given Romney the go-ahead he needed to invade Washington, Oregon, California and Nevada and schedule as many games as he could, provided the games were completed before classes started again in January. It was Romney's big opportunity, and by November 10, he had lined up an almost impossible eighteen games for the tour. It would mean the team would play or travel almost every day, with only a break on Christmas Day, which would be celebrated wherever they happened to be on the road.

On December 16, eight members of the Bobcat basketball team boarded the westbound train in Bozeman, including key players Valery Glynn and Adolph Hartwig. Brick Breeden was along, and they were in the company of their determined coach, Ott Romney, and student manager, "Little Joe"

1929 Basketball National Champions

Alfred Atkinson, president of Montana State College from 1919 to 1935. *Courtesy Montana State University Library Special Collections.*

Ottenheimer. Money was in short supply, and sadly, the team had to leave behind some of the bench players, as well as Assistant Coach Schubert Dyche, who had been a vital part of getting the team in condition for the trip. Nevertheless, as the train chugged out of Bozeman, those onboard were cautiously optimistic, even though they were destined to travel 3,500 miles in the next twenty-six days.[108]

The next day, the Bobcats stepped off the train in Moscow, Idaho, and walked up a gradual slope to the University of Idaho campus and its gymnasium amid the Gothic-styled neighboring campus buildings. They observed the rolling hills outside of town and knew they were out of the mountains and onto the great Palouse, that wild-horse prairie of rolling hills that spread west across eastern Washington for a hundred miles or more.

The game that night against Idaho was typical of the times—slow and low-scoring—with the teams evenly matched, but the Bobcats lost, 28–24. It was just the kind of game Romney didn't want from his offense, which was unable to score proficiently. The next day, the Bobcats made the short ten-mile trip across the state line to Pullman to take on Washington State College, and they lost again, 35–30. The trip had not started well. A dispirited Bobcat team then got back on the train bound for Seattle, where they played two independent teams, beating the Seattle Amateur Athletic Club, 38–26, and the Tacoma Athletic Club, 30–21.[109] The team then moved on again, and two days later, the Bobcats were in the sunshine of California to play the University of the Pacific, the state's oldest chartered institution.[110] This time, even though their shots were not falling at the rate they wanted, the Bobcat defense frustrated the Tigers to give the Cats a 31–22 victory. As Romney thought about the win, he knew it was due in large part to the stellar defensive play of freshman Brick Breeden. In the warm California winter climate, at least some things were starting to look better.

The Bobcats moved south down the tracks and played the University of California in Berkeley and lost, 36–21, again not hitting their shots. They were also beaten, 24–21, by Whittier College, a powerhouse in the sprawling Los Angeles area. Then they played Loyola College on its Los Angeles campus atop the bluffs overlooking the Pacific Ocean. They won resoundingly, 49–17, finally showing the promise Ott Romney expected to see. Then they were matched up against the Long Beach Athletic Club, a class outfit that played competitively in the California AAU leagues, and won, 24–21. The Bobcats won again the next night against another good team, the Alhambra Athletic Club, 23–17. What Romney was learning in each game was the value of having Breeden back on defense. With him there, Ott could commit both Glynn and Hartwig to the offensive game.[111]

With their revamped style starting to emerge, the Bobcats were in a confident mood when they got off the train in Reno, where they played two games against the University of Nevada, a tough team. They won them both by close scores, 31–30 and 20–17. Again, they relied on the strength of Breeden's defense, which compensated for their own poor shooting the second night and had been a key to the win the first night. Then it was back on the train again across the Great Basin of northern Nevada and on to Pocatello, Idaho, where the Bobcats played Idaho Technical College—which had not yet become Idaho State College—and won, 27–16, in the home team's Reed Hall. It was then back on the train to Bozeman. Once back in town, they played the Montana Normal School from Dillon and the Montana State School of Mines from Butte, scoring 40 in the first game but only 32 in the second. The now proven freshman Brick Breeden and the defense held the teams to 13 points each.

A few days later, the Bobcats took the floor in front of a sellout crowd in Bozeman to open the Rocky Mountain Conference season. They were playing the eventual conference winners, the Utah State Aggies, coached by Ott's younger brother Dick Romney. This was the game the team had been looking forward to, as it would test whether Ott's early season strategy of a barnstorming tour and his new team alignment had achieved the results he expected. They learned that it had not happened yet. When the first game started, both teams came out strong, with the lead changing several times. At the half, the score was 18–17 in favor of the Aggies. In the second half, things changed. The Bobcats couldn't get in position fast enough to stop the relentless shooting of the visitors. This, coupled with an increase in defensive pressure, led to Utah Aggie victories, 35–30 in the first game and 40–23 on the next night. The Bobcats were still learning.[112]

When the University of Utah basketball team came to Bozeman, it arrived with big, muscular players. Their wide bodies made it hard for Hartwig to get around them on drives to the basket from the high post. But the aggressive defense and long arms of Brick Breeden stifled them, and the Utes could score only 23 points. Alas, the Bobcats were worse, and in a loss they managed only 22 points. The next night, Ott Romney and the Bobcats arrived at the gymnasium early for shooting practice; by game time, the shots were falling and the mood of the team had turned positive. Ott had once again given them the encouragement they needed, and some who watched the game said every player on the team was like a fighting tornado. Adolph Hartwig was energized and made shots over the Utes to lead the Bobcats to a 39–28 win.[113]

The games the rest of the season, all against Rocky Mountain Conference teams, were not that successful, with the Bobcats and their opponents averaging low offensive outputs, nearly 30 points a game. The Bobcats finished the conference with just six wins and eight losses. More work needed to be done.

After the season, Ott and Schubert had long talks about getting the right new recruits to fill the available spots the next year. They didn't want to just wait and see who showed up on campus to go out for the team when practices started. They had of course been aware of the Montana players who would be coming out of high school, but they had to compete for them with the university in Missoula, which had won out on many occasions. To get the full complement of skills they needed, Ott and Schubert had to open the field to players from both in and out of state.[114]

When their discussions turned to the attributes they were looking for in new players, Ott and Schubert agreed that speed was the main thing. They were looking for more scoring than what came out of the traditional game, in which the ball was sometimes passed again and again around the perimeter until it wound up with a man who had become open for a flat-

Basketball from the Dixie High School display case in St. George, Utah, from the Chicago Interscholastic Tournament in 1925. Early basketballs were made of seamed leather with heavy laces closing an opening where an inflation tube was covered. The laces caused the ball to bounce erratically, making dribbling less popular then it later became. *Dixie High School, St. George, Utah. Author's collection.*

footed set shot. These games could result in scores of 30 points or fewer, and Ott and Schubert agreed that this offensive output could be doubled to around 60 points per game with the right players, as long as they were fast. Their team would win with offense, rather than relying mostly on defense. Besides, with Brick Breeden coming back, they had one of basketball's best defenders. This year, they could concentrate on scorers.

The Bobcat coaches were also looking for a dribbler who could make the best use of the new basketballs, which had concealed valves and laces. The new balls were less likely to carom off in the wrong direction and easier to dribble with successive bounces, enabling a player to go all the way down the court with the ball, sometimes catching a defense off guard as they penetrated toward the basket. However, dribbling a lot was not universally popular, and in 1926, Coach Dan Meenan of Columbia University voiced his opinion that he didn't like it at all, "because it momentarily ties up the other four men on the team." He advised, "Never dribble…unless you are coming up to the basket for a shot and there's no one in front of you." It was his opinion that the opponents had a hard time keeping track of the ball if it was passed; in a dribbling game, "on the other hand, every opponent knows exactly where the ball is."[115]

13

THE BROTHERS

Frank Ward and Orland Ward of Parowan, Utah

> *Oh, P.H.S. we love thee best of all*
> *The schools in Southern Utah*
> *We shout thy name, we hail thy fame,*
> *We love thee best of all.*
>
> *(Sung to "Farewell to Thee")*[116]

Along the small farm road leading west out of Parowan, Utah, two teenage boys who could hear the high school theme song in their heads were walking with purposeful strides. They talked little, intent instead on passing a basketball back and forth between them, sometimes bouncing it on the hard-packed dirt road. They were the Ward brothers. Frank was the older brother—quieter, taller and more erect, with the stride and strength of a mature athlete. Orland was the younger. He was developing to be as well-muscled as his brother but shorter and more active. They had just come from basketball practice at the gym attached to the local high school in the small southern Utah town.

As they walked home, the brothers were hardly aware of the low sun streaming through a gap in the sandstone hills some eight miles to the northwest of their small valley town. The eerie shadows it produced were sent racing across the sagebrush slope, gradually leading down to a hamlet of modest houses, outskirt farms, dirt roads, small stores, an impressive Mormon

Frank and Orland Ward as teenagers in Parowan, Utah. *Courtesy Wendy Lisonbee, from Frank Ward family photographs.*

tabernacle and two Protestant churches. The town had been named Parowan after an Indian tribe that had once inhabited the region. The walls of the gap through which the Indians—and then later the Mormon settlers—had passed were decorated with petroglyphs of different periods, carved into the rock by the Indians.

In the 1920s, Parowan had a population of around fifteen hundred. The center of interest for many of the townspeople was the new basketball gym, built just a few years prior as part of the town's small high school of around one hundred students.[117] Home games were filled with cheering spectators who stood while the school song was sung.

Frank Ward became absorbed with basketball at a young age, and he grew up hearing a lot about a great player from the town. It was Alma Richards, the son of a local grocer. Alma had played there in the 1900s and had been such a good player that people still talked about him, but what they really talked about was his almost unbelievable athletic fame. He won the decathlon in the 1912 Stockholm Olympics.[118] Alma had dropped out of school in Parowan at fourteen after the eighth grade, when he had already grown to a strapping six feet, two inches tall and weighed over two hundred pounds. A boy that big could do a man's job, so he worked both on the land and in his father's store. Then, at age nineteen, he went to the private Murdock Academy in the town of Beaver, up the road about forty miles. There he became a one-man track team, scoring enough points by himself in the Salt Lake City state meet to win the championship for his small school. After graduating with honors from Cornell University, he attended graduate school at Stanford University before studying law at the University of Southern California. He got his law degree, and the locals joked that "like high jumpers do, he passed the bar."[119]

Frank Ward grew up as a clone of Alma Richards. He was big, strong and athletic when he was just fourteen. Also like Alma, he had dropped out of school to do work. Ever since he was eleven years old he had been aware of his own athletic abilities and frequently heard himself compared to

1929 Basketball National Champions

Frank Ward *(front row, center)* with Parowan High School team. *Courtesy Parowan High School.*

Richards. Alma's example had shown Frank Ward that a good athlete could also be a good student, something Frank's future coaches would approve of.

In 1920, when Frank returned to school as a freshman at Parowan High, he was already seventeen years old. He was twenty-one when he graduated in 1924 as a mature, confident and intelligent young man with great athletic ability. His younger brother Orland was a sophomore that year, and he, too, had dropped out of school for a time to help on the family acreage. They took farming seriously, and in 1917, Frank was given a blue ribbon at the county fair some twenty miles to the south in the bigger town of Cedar City for growing the best cabbage.[120]

In March 1924, when Frank and Orland were playing basketball for Parowan High, they had gone to the state tournament in Salt Lake City as one of the sixteen teams invited. Parowan was one of the smaller schools, but that didn't deter them, and Frank and Orland Ward and their teammates arrived there by train to compete as best they could. In the eyes of the farm boys from Iron County, going into the large neoclassical Deseret Gym was scary.

Once inside the building, the boys headed for the dressing rooms and quickly changed into their uniforms. As they came out into the main arena with its floor of polished maple, they could see the competing team entering and hear a round of applause coming from the large big-city crowds in the spectator gallery. The fewer fans from Parowan could hardly be located. Fans or no fans, Parowan had a good basketball team led by Frank Ward in his junior year, and they took fourth place. When the team played Springville, the players were not given much respect. One biased reporter said, "In tonight's games Springville should be able to take the scalp of the Parowan boys."[121] It didn't happen, and Parowan placed in the tournament.

Back home, when Frank was approaching his twenty-second birthday, the town of Parowan was starting to notice his attraction to the striking, dark-haired Mary Esther Green, the daughter of the prominent Dr. Green. Some noticed that Frank was trying to seek the favor of Mary's father, and the *Parowan Times* reported, "Mr. Frank Ward did a very fine job of removing the weeds and cleaning up the sidewalk in front of Dr. Green's residence."[122] The *Iron County Record* in Cedar City liked to seize on rumors and pass them on with colorful innuendo. Mary's father was the subject of many stories, and he was fair game, because of his flamboyant lifestyle. In 1913, when Mary would have been eight years old, the paper noted that Green "was seen going through town on a motorcycle at a rate something less than 90 miles an hour."[123]

The romance blossomed from the start. Mary was not a Mormon, but that didn't make a difference. Her father was a staunch Presbyterian and had worked with other Protestants and some Mormon friends in the construction of a wooden church.[124] This was the culmination of a program the Presbyterians had started as far back as 1896, when the church leaders met in New York. It was reported that Utah, which had just become a state, had only twenty-three Presbyterian churches and twenty-five ministers. As they said, "Away from the centers of light and of American influence the old Mormon growl is distinctly heard."[125] Be they Mormons or non-Mormons, the young people of the small town of Parowan were not concerned, and much activity was open to everyone.[126]

In an age when it was popular for almost every high school and college student to have a nickname, Frank picked up "Huzzy" as his. About the time he graduated from high school, it had become institutionalized in the regional papers. Not everyone knew for sure what it meant, but that didn't matter.

When graduation day came for Frank Ward in Parowan, he was not there. A state track meet in Ogden was more important, and from there he went directly to the state of Oregon, where he had found work for the summer, arranged for him by a relative. By the end of July, Frank had caught a ride back to Parowan. He could once again turn his attentions to Mary Green.[127]

1929 Basketball National Champions

Frank Ward running track. *1930* Montanan.

Frank was naturally competitive and had found another new interest. Of all things, it was boxing. After Frank had been in enough matches to know he was good, he believed he was quick and strong enough to overpower almost any of the opponents, some by knockout, in his town, as well as in Cedar City, which held matches at the summer fairs. His younger brother Orland shared his bravery but not his skill, and when Orland got in the ring at the fair, he was knocked out "in about 27 seconds" by Lynn Hunter of Cedar City, who swung wildly and landed. That didn't sit well with the Ward family. The next night, a revenge match of six rounds between Hunter and Frank Ward was billed as the chief attraction of the night's program. In the first round, Hunter was put down to the mat; early in the second, he was knocked out when Frank landed on the point of his chin.[128]

In the fall, the students at Parowan High were glad to see that Orland Ward had survived his short boxing career and was back. He was named president of his junior class, with Mary Green serving on the executive committee. At the end of October, the students divided into two parties, the "Climbers" and the "Boosters," and held schoolwide elections. The nominee of the Boosters for the highest office of chief commissioner was Frank Ward. For the Climbers, Orland Ward was nominated as commissioner of discipline—something the opposition would say he had little of. They also nominated Mary as commissioner of amusements, something all agreed the popular girl had plenty of qualifications for.

Having graduated from high school, Frank Ward drove the twenty miles to Cedar City to enroll in Branch Agricultural College. Known by the acronym BAC, the two-year junior college was part of the Utah State Agricultural College in Logan. In his family, Frank was the first member to go beyond high school; some of his siblings had dropped out of school after the eighth grade. Faculty and students quickly welcomed him there, and he immediately became the star player of the basketball team. In the BAC student election on November 5, he won the post of commissioner of athletics.[129]

In the spring of 1925, Frank led the BAC basketball team in Utah's junior-college tournament. He performed well, but when he was away from the basketball games, the fans from Cedar City and Parowan could tell something was on his mind. Usually friendly and receptive and not at all shy about talking to young women, Frank had gone silent. The *Iron County*

Frank Ward (*to the left of the coach*) with Branch Agricultural College team. *Courtesy Southern Utah University Library Archives.*

Record tried to explain it—with a humor that Frank did not share. He was about to embark on one of the most serious things in his life. Under the headline "'Huzz' Ward Is Snared for Life," the paper reported that Frank "has succumbed to the wiles of matrimony." "Well, it's probably all right. Huzz had good judgment on hoops and distance and things. His choice isn't questioned (in fact what is good enough for Frank Ward has a good ring to most everyone), but the fact is lamented that the chances for him back at center next year are greatly lessened." As to his behavior, the paper reported, "It's strange…that he should appear such an 'aloofer' from the opposite sex at the tournament and visit the parson so soon after—maybe not so strange."[130] Frank Ward and Mary Green were married in El Segundo, California, on Monday evening at the home of the bride's uncle.[131]

The marriage was lamented by BAC sports fans, who thought this meant the end to Frank's basketball career. Rumors flew that the bride was expecting, and they were true. A baby, James Frank Ward, was born on June 20, 1925. Parenthood did not stop Frank or Mary, and he stayed in school. The next fall, he enrolled again for what he thought would be the final year of his college basketball career. Little did he know then that the participation of his team in the spring in a junior-college tournament would put him in touch with his future college coaches. They would pave his way to All-American fame with the Montana State College Golden Bobcat team.[132]

14

THE RECRUITING OF
THE GOLDEN BOBCATS

At center Coach Romney probably will start Frank Ward a tall and fast yearling of outstanding promise....Gilbert McFarland, former star of the Billings high team, and Ashworth Thompson, another new player are prominent candidates for forward positions.
—Independent Record, *December 20, 1926*

In March 1926, Montana State College assistant coach Schubert Dyche got his first chance to see Cat Thompson and Frank Ward play, in Ogden in the Utah state junior-college tournament. Ward played for Branch Agricultural Junior College of Cedar City, and Thompson played for Dixie Junior College of St. George. What got Dyche there was a stop by the Bobcats in Ogden on their way to play Utah State in Logan after playing Utah University in Salt Lake City. Matched in the junior-college tournament were Ricks College from Rexburg, Idaho; LDS College from Logan, Utah; Weber College from Ogden, the host of the tournament; Dixie College from St. George in southern Utah; and Branch Agricultural College from Cedar City. An oddity was that LDS in Logan was affiliated with BYU, while BAC in Cedar City was affiliated with Utah State in Logan.

Dyche had been sent to the tournament by Ott Romney, who had picked up a copy of the *Ogden Standard-Examiner* and read accounts of the previous night's tournament games. He and Schubert hurriedly considered the matter. It was decided that Dyche would stay in Ogden to scout the junior-college teams with the barest glimmer of hope that a better player—or maybe even more than one—would want to come to Montana State if they were "encouraged." Schubert would have to be cautious, because athletic scholarships were neither available nor sanctioned by the conference, and the players were supposed to come on their own money. Ott himself had transferred to Montana State to play a fourth year of college. He had been at Utah, where he was ineligible to play a fourth year because he had already graduated there. He knew the uproar that had ensued when coaches in Utah and in Missoula at Montana State University had claimed he was being paid to play.

There was also a question of eligibility and whether the transfers would lose the years they were playing in junior college. There were also counterarguments, and some thought junior colleges should be treated as prep schools with no college credits being transferred. Several times, the conference had referred the issue for study by a committee of the members, but they never really reported back with concrete recommendations, and the conference's minutes did not reflect any definite action.[133] The only guidance Romney could give to Schubert was to tell him to introduce himself to any outstanding players he thought had enough talent and at least let them know that someone from Montana State had watched their games and was impressed with their play.

Waiting for the evening's games, Schubert sat in the lobby of the St. Paul Hotel in Ogden where he had taken a room for the night. He picked up the *Ogden Standard-Examiner*. Spotting the headline "Southern Quints Boast Fast Teams," he settled down to read an account of the Dixie College and Branch Agricultural College squads. The two teams had tied for first-place honors in the southern junior-college sector with two victories and one defeat each. The teams had split their two games against each other, with BAC winning at Cedar City and Dixie winning at St. George.[134]

Schubert was aware that on the first night of the tournament BAC had lost, 28–26, to LDS Junior College, somewhat to the surprise of the crowd. But Frank Ward was able to score 18 points. The Dixie Flyers had taken a narrow 27–24 game against BYU Junior College, with Thompson scoring 15 points.

When Schubert arrived early in the evening, a ticket for one dollar got him a reserved seat close to the floor. The BAC game was starting against Weber, and he soon recognized the extraordinary ability of Frank Ward, who rebounded and ran the floor and shot from both underneath and outside. His teammates were not providing much help, and he was up against a large, stocky center who used his body and hands to push Frank away from the basket. But it didn't make much difference, and Ward scored 21 points, many coming on put-backs as he soared above his grabbing opponent. Despite his output, Frank was not even the high scorer in the game, which hung in the balance at the end as Frank missed a shot under the basket, rebounded and missed again as the buzzer went off. Weber was the winner. In another game that evening, Ashworth Thompson and his Dixie Flyers were defeated soundly by Ricks, 34–24, with Thompson scoring only 8 points; the accolades went to a teammate who had 10. The Flyers played listlessly, and the underdog Ricks had taken advantage.[135]

Dixie College went head-to-head with BAC the next night. The tournament championship was not on the line for either team—BAC had already lost two games, and Dixie had lost one. What was on the line was the informal, mythical championship of the southern Utah region. The notable matchup that Schubert watched was the battle of the two centers, which initially looked like a mismatch. The Dixie Flyers' center was Thompson, who was only five feet, nine inches tall, about a half foot shorter than Frank Ward of BAC. Schubert marveled at Thompson's catlike quickness and his ability to disrupt the other team. His moves were lightning fast, and a few in the stands were even calling him "Cat." He had been put at the center position by his coach because he had the ability to contest Frank Ward. When Frank pivoted to drive to the basket, he would find Thompson in his way. When Frank stepped back to take a jump shot, Cat would be there and jump high enough to disrupt the shot. When Frank held the ball and then tried to pass to a teammate cutting to the basket, Cat could sometimes deflect the ball.

It was about that time that Schubert started to develop an idea. He could envision a player like Thompson in a more natural forward position playing with a man like Frank Ward on the same team to form a twosome that would have outstanding scoring ability. It didn't take Dyche long to realize that Ashworth Thompson and Frank Ward were players he and Ott Romney would like to have in Bozeman.[136]

After the game, Schubert approached Frank Ward on the floor. If nothing else, Schubert wanted to introduce himself and say he sincerely admired Frank's play. He had found out from talking to Branch AC fans at the hotel and in the stands at the game that Frank had been married over a year before and that he and his wife, Mary, had a baby child. To Schubert, the chances of moving an entire family to Bozeman did not look good, but he thought it was worth a try. With a good deal of trepidation, but in his usual straightforward manner, Schubert went up to the big center and introduced himself as the assistant coach at Montana State. Somewhat to his surprise, he found Frank friendly and glad to meet him. In addition, Frank was appreciative of the direct questions about his future. Frank answered truthfully that he really didn't know what he was going to do. Mary and the baby were his first responsibility, and he expected he would get a job and settle down in Utah. Schubert parted with the comment that either Schubert or Coach Ott Romney might try to get in touch with him if they thought he could fit in at Montana State. A big question was whether Frank's wife and baby would be able to move to Bozeman and be comfortable. Only Frank and Mary could answer that question.

Schubert Dyche was also able to get to Cat Thompson on the floor and introduce himself as being from Montana State. Few words were spoken. Schubert left things with the fact that he was interested in talking to Cat again sometime. Dyche had been complimentary and said just enough so that Cat would remember him for his sincerity.

With the tournament games over, it was no surprise that Frank Ward was named captain and center of the first all-tournament team. For that, he was awarded a watch. What didn't make any sense was that Thompson made only the second team at center. The *Ogden Standard-Examiner* noted that the all-tournament team of 1926 was chosen strictly by position, and Ashworth, who the paper thought was the second-best player in the tournament, was stuck at the position behind Frank Ward. This was even in the face of Cat's final night's performance. As the Examiner noted, "Thompson went wild on the final night by caging 12 baskets from the court."[137]

Frank Ward felt somewhat encouraged by what he had heard from Schubert Dyche, and when he got back to Cedar City he started to think about his future. A college education was not in the tradition of the Wards, who were farmers. However, the advantages of higher education had become known and offered alternatives for many farm boys. Frank had gone to Branch Agricultural College so he could play basketball, but he also liked to learn and did well academically, enough that he was confident he could obtain a four-year degree if he had the opportunity. Above all, he wanted to continue to play more basketball.

On the train from Utah back to Bozeman, Ott and Schubert spent a lot of time talking about the potential of both Frank Ward and Cat Thompson. They also talked about the junior-college eligibility question, which vexed Ott. From what he was hearing, the Utah colleges were mired in a combination of conference rules, in-state Utah rules and gentlemen's agreements that would give Frank Ward only two years of eligibility if he

Sigma Chi fraternity, MSC. *1930* Montanan.

transferred to any of the state's three campuses. He might even have to sit out a year before playing there. Would the situation be the same if they came to Montana State? Romney set out in earnest to find the answer. It turned out to be a simple solution. Montana State did not have any separate understandings with the Utah colleges and could ignore entirely the junior-college attendance in Utah and treat it as if it was attendance at a prep school. The two players would be enrolled as freshmen, starting anew in their college coursework. No credits would be transferred, and like true freshmen athletes coming in, they would be enrolled in the usual first-year courses and have four years of college eligibility.

    The next morning, after Ott and Schubert got back, Ott walked up the stairs in Montana Hall to meet with President Atkinson and Deane Swingle, Montana State's Rocky Mountain Conference faculty representative. Romney's proposal seemed overly simplified and perhaps somewhat extreme, but he presented it anyway, and Atkinson liked it. He gave Romney the go-ahead to see if he could somehow get the players interested in the idea. From the players' standpoint, it would be a tradeoff: receive

1929 Basketball National Champions

MSC President Alfred Atkinson. *1930 Montanan.*

four years of college basketball and give up the academic work they had already done at their junior colleges that might have been accepted for college credit elsewhere.[138]

The decision was made that Frank Ward and Cat Thompson could be approached during the summer, but that it should not be by Ott Romney. There was no use in stirring up the bad blood that had existed when he had come to Montana State from Utah as a player in 1914. Instead, Schubert Dyche, who many sports fans in Salt Lake City liked to remember as just a janitor, was given the task. He would embark in the summer heat on the seven-hundred-mile drive to southern Utah to make the contacts.

By the summer of 1926, Frank, as a married twenty-two-year-old, had almost given up on going further in college, and he had found a job he really liked. He was employed by the Union Pacific Railway as a "gandy dancer," laying railroad tracks. He worked out of Milford, Utah, some fifty miles from Parowan. What had sold him on the job was the opportunity to participate with the Milford Athletic Club in the railway's track-and-field competitions held at locations along its lengthy line. He won at meets held in Utah and Los Angeles, and in early September, he boarded the train for Cheyenne, Wyoming, to participate in the biggest meet of its kind west of the Mississippi, with over three hundred athletes competing. In his previous meet, in California, he had taken first in the high jump, the 120-yard hurdles, the 220 low hurdles, the 440- and 880-yard relays and the 16-pound shot put. He placed second in the javelin and discus. If he won in Cheyenne, he would go on to a national meet in Philadelphia the next month.[139] Visions of his idol, Alma Richards, going to the Olympics started to appear, and Frank, a big winner in the track meets, began to think that he could be headed that way. But fate intervened.

Schubert Dyche, on his long trip south to La Verkin in southern Utah and back to Bozeman, had also stopped in Parowan with the message that Ott

Montana State's Golden Bobcats

Parowan High School 1926 basketball team. Orland Ward is standing to the left of the coach. *Courtesy Parowan High School.*

Romney wanted Frank Ward to come to Montana State and play basketball. It would be on the condition that he was willing to start college all over again as a true freshman and have four years of eligibility. Deep down, Frank wanted to continue using his talents in basketball for as long as he could, and he also wanted a college education. It was the best of both worlds: four more years of basketball and, at the end, a college degree from a recognized university, even though it was far to the north in Montana. He was starting to realize that his dreams may have just come true.

Schubert was also able to tell Frank Ward that his competitor, Ashworth Thompson of Dixie College in St. George, might also be coming to Montana State as a freshman. This was nothing but good news to Frank, as he had admired Cat's play and looked forward to teaming with him.

Before telling Schubert Dyche definitely that he would be coming to Bozeman, Frank had one condition. Frank's brother Orland had just graduated from high school and, while not as tall, mature and accomplished as Frank, had shown promise. Orland believed he could be a college basketball player. He wanted to come along. If that is what it was going to take to get Frank to Montana, Schubert Dyche was sure Ott Romney would give him a chance.

15

TRIP TO MONTANA

In the summer of 1867, General Alfred Terry of the U.S. Army had visited Montana Territory at the request of General William Tecumseh Sherman. He had gone first to Virginia City, then Helena, and then on to the fledgling town of Bozeman with its 160 inhabitants. As he rode into the broad agricultural valley…he observed the steep mountain range to the east which he could see would serve as a natural fortress.
—From Paul R. Wylie, Blood on the Marias[140]

For Frank and Mary Ward, it was an optimistic drive to a new future in a new state. With them were their toddler son, Jimmy, and Frank's brother Orland. Cat Thompson caravanned with them in another car driven by Joe Ottenheimer. They knew they were facing challenges, including the long, cold winters in Montana, and they were ready to accept them for the opportunities that lay ahead.

The northbound road they were on left Utah and went into Idaho, where a few hours' drive brought them to the Snake River, which they crossed on a bridge above the roaring waters at Idaho Falls. They then proceeded north on the last leg of their trip. The route was over fertile, flat farmland. Ahead of them, a thin blue line was starting to appear on the northern horizon. As they drove farther, they could see the first of the lower mountain ranges that separated the high valleys of Montana from the plains of Idaho. To Thompson and the Wards, it would hold more than just geographical significance, as the mountains separated the domains of the Latter-day Saint culture, in which they had been raised, from the largely Irish Catholic miners of Butte and the staid Protestants of the Gallatin Valley. LDS churches almost did not exist in this northern country.[141]

When Joe Ottenheimer's car came down a winding road and out onto the Gallatin Valley floor only a few miles from Bozeman, the beauty of the mountains was evident, and the quiet town fit well into the scene. Ashworth Thompson was impressed. The town had now grown to a population of around four thousand and was home to Montana State College with its seven hundred students and impressive new buildings, including one of the most beautiful gymnasiums Cat would ever see. He was a long way from home, but he was going to stake his future here, and there was no turning back. Ottenheimer drove Cat to the Sigma Chi house on Bozeman's finest street, tree-lined South Willson Avenue, where Ott Romney was faculty advisor and had arranged for Thompson to live, with a strong suggestion that he might want to be initiated into the fraternity soon. The same suggestion was made to Frank and Orland Ward, even though they would not be living in the fraternity house.[142][143] Frank, Mary and young Jimmy, along with Orland, arrived in their own car and moved into a basement apartment about eight blocks from the campus, at 607 Seventh Avenue South.

The Southern Utah group, from left to right: Orland Ward, Frank Ward and Ashworth "Cat" Thompson. *Montana State University*.

After a few days, the Utah transplants set out to explore their new environs. As they had come from the rural communities in Southern Utah, Bozeman struck them as somewhat upscale. According to published information, there were "a number of new, modern apartment houses of the finest type, the largest of which are the Blackmore, the Evergreen, the Clark and Bridger Arms." Amusements were plentiful, with two beautiful and modern theaters, the Ellen and the Rialto; a nine-hole golf course; parks; a playground; and wonderful scenic drives. There was also hunting, fishing and many summer resorts up the Gallatin River Canyon.[144]

Walking through the Montana State campus on a beautiful September day, Cat Thompson and the Ward boys discovered a small pond and ducks swimming there, and it brought to mind the marshes around Parowan.[145] The duck pond was lined with a few benches, and on that warm fall day, some of the new female students who had stepped out of their residence in Hamilton Hall, farther up the hill to the east, were talking and watching the young men on campus. It was a matter of little interest to Frank Ward, who had brought his young wife to Bozeman. The girls were of considerable interest to Orland and of guarded interest to Thompson, who was thinking only of basketball.

As the boys walked back up the hill to the east, they could see the spires of Montana Hall, where Alfred Atkinson, the president of Montana State College, held court. Built in 1903, the hall's cornerstone had been laid some years earlier. Then there was the classic Italianate engineering building, in place since three years before, in 1923, and an ornate chemistry building just above the duck pond, completed in 1919. But the crown jewel was the new gymnasium, with its Italian Renaissance architecture. It was more beautiful and even a tiny bit larger than the Deseret Gym in Salt Lake City. Frank Ward, in particular, had previously thought of the Deseret as the finest sports facility he would ever see, but not anymore.[146]

Already, the familiar fall sounds of a football practice on the fields south of the gym could be heard on campus, with the occasional thump of a ball being kicked and the shouts of the players as they urged on their teammates. It wasn't too many days before the trio from Utah checked out uniforms and pads and showed up on the field to give the sport a try. But it wasn't really their interest, and Ott Romney didn't want them injured before the basketball season even started, so they soon dropped out of the practices. By that time, classes had started, and Cat Thompson realized the challenges of taking the tough curricula at Montana State; he needed all the time available to study.[147]

True to their understanding with Schubert Dyche, both Frank and Cat were enrolled as beginning freshmen. Even though the men had taken basic college courses at their junior colleges, it was not easy for them when they were met by demanding professors who had their own ideas about learning. Schubert Dyche had told both of them to bring their junior-college transcripts along and take them to Montana Hall, where the registrar, Roy Orvis Wilson, happened to be on the faculty committee for eligibility for athletics. He looked the transcripts over and told the boys to come back later. When they did, Cat Thompson was listed as having 58 quarter-hours of advanced standing college credit. Frank Ward, who had attended two years at Branch Agricultural College, had been given only 29 advanced standing credits. Despite this, they started out taking the normal freshman-year classes: English, math, history, et cetera. It wasn't until the end of his college years, when Frank Ward didn't have enough credits to meet the minimum of 216 quarter-hours needed for graduation, that his advanced standing credits from BAC were used, allowing him to graduate. Cat Thompson, the better student of the two, graduated after only three years and stayed on for a fourth in a different major.[148]

Frank Ward. *Courtesy Wendy Lisonbee from Frank Ward family photographs.*

Apart from meeting their academic demands, time was spent by the basketball players in the magnificent gymnasium, where they could practice every afternoon. They played pickup games, played horse, dribbled on the shining floor, took shots off the backboards and dreamed of winning a starting position on the Bobcat basketball team, something expected to happen but not guaranteed. Mary Ward would come to the practices and watch from the stands and marvel how well Frank and Ashworth played together. She remembered first seeing the agile and inventive Thompson play against her husband back when Dixie High School came north about seventy miles to play Parowan, It was the game that drew the interest of the Parowan fans in the small, young, blond-haired man from St. George with the determined expression. Mary was also encouraged when she saw her brother-in-law, Orland, beginning to play better in practice, making more shots, defending against Thompson and pairing with his brother on some spectacular plays.

16

1926–27 SEASON

"What's the Matter with Our School Spirit."
—*Montana State College* Exponent, *November 2, 1926*

In its editorial, the Montana State College student paper, the *Exponent*, said that what was needed was "a revival of spirit to a sufficient pitch to keep the cheering increasing as the team decreases in fight or success on an ever increasing scale so that the enthusiasm of the crowd on the stands will electrify the players and put them into a fight spirit of mind." During the season, the Bobcat basketball team got the spirit. They would play thirty-seven games, winning thirty. The age of the "Golden Bobcats" was about to dawn.[149]

In the fall of 1926, something unusual was starting to happen on the Bozeman campus. The student body was finding a voice, and the administration was dealing with some student unrest. A national fear of the spread of communism had reached the college. In another movement, pacifists in the student body were staging protests—complete with signboards and speeches—against the teaching of military science on campus. While the matters died down in time, the editors of the *Exponent* said the protest may have expressed the true emotions of its proponents that war was wrong and should be eliminated. Awareness and interest in a broad range of things was beginning to show.

In that same edition of the *Exponent* there appeared a preview of the team for the upcoming basketball season. Back from the previous year were two outstanding players, guard Brick Breeden and Val Glynn. People seemed to know that Glynn would no longer be playing center. Frank Ward and Cat Thompson were listed as "new men with exceptional ability and with good high school records." Missing was the fact that the two had also played at junior colleges.[150] It was also announced that Romney was continuing a barnstorming ambition. The new team would leave on December 17, after classes were over for the fall quarter, to play nineteen games with teams on the west side of the Rocky Mountains and on the Pacific coast. They would get back to Bozeman on January 7, just in time to start winter quarter classes and prepare for the tough Rocky Mountain Conference schedule.

After playing two one-sided exhibition games against the Livingston Railway team, the Bobcats left on the train going west over the Continental Divide to face stiff competition. Their planned nineteen-game trip had already been cut to twelve games after some of the expected opponents bowed out. But Washington State, the 1917 national champion, was eagerly waiting for them in Pullman. The Cougars were still a formidable opponent, beating the Bobcats, 38–35, in the first game and narrowly losing to them, 31–28, in the second.[151]

It was then just a short eight-mile drive back over the state line to Moscow, Idaho, where the Bobcats lost the first game to the University of Idaho Vandals, 31–28. The Bobcats had a bad night. Many of them were too inexperienced to know that the excitement of being on the road in new places had to be controlled in favor of a regular discipline of sleep, good meals and enough exercise and warm-up drills to keep their bodies tuned. The loss bothered Cat Thompson as much as anyone on the team, except perhaps the uncompromising Romney, who outlined a new strategy for the Bobcats in the second game. The Bobcats still shot cold in the beginning, then Romney gave the green light for Thompson to start shooting. The result was five straight baskets before the half ended in a 18–15 lead for the Bobcats, with a bewildered Idaho team wondering what hit them. Never had they seen such a quick display of variety and accuracy. Soon after the second half started, the Bobcats widened the lead to 9 points on scoring by Frank Ward, who started to go over and around his defender. That player was soon replaced by one with more skill, but he was playing in his first game, and it was too late. The Bobcats' fantastic freshmen, Ward and Thompson, actually had just 10 points each, but the defensive attention they attracted freed up other players to contribute. The Bobcats also scored 14 points on free throws, as the Vandals tried to stop them by grabbing and hacking. The final score was 38–29.[152]

1929 Basketball National Champions

A whirlwind of games followed. The Bobcats moved on to Spokane, Washington, the next night to defeat a good team from Whitman College, 33–31, and then again a day later, 32–19. The offense was not yet gelling, but Brick Breeden and the defense were holding down their opponents. Two more games in the state of Washington yielded victories over the Potlach Athletic Club, 40–32, and then the Toppenish Athletic Club, 55–18, followed by a win over the Yakima, Washington YMCA, 62–21. Then it was still another victory, this time 42–31 over a team sponsored by Brothers Bank. While these teams had players with experience, they were not in the physical condition required to stay with the Bobcats, who were starting to run.

It was then on to the University of Washington to play the Huskies in their old gymnasium, which was in its last year. Plans were in place to replace it in 1927 with what would become Hec Edmundson Pavilion, still in use today. The Bobcats were now getting to know one another's abilities, and they came out running and passing to win the first game, 43–34. They shot poorly the second night, and while holding the tall Huskies again to 34 points, they could score only 29 themselves. Romney's goal of having his team average 60 points a game was still a long way off.

Back in Bozeman, with a brief time off for Christmas, the Bobcats were ready to play in their own gym. They had seen the facilities of famous, bigger universities, and they were proud that their building was the equal of any of them. They knew their team, unproven as yet, could be a match for any team on their schedule. The Bobcats knew they would have to prove that against top-flight teams but in the meantime they played down and beat Jamestown University of North Dakota, 59–18 and 44–15, on successive nights. A week later, they embarrassed Montana Mines, 59–15, and then had an 81–8 victory over the team from Montana Normal in Dillon.

Ott Romney and his team were now ready for the Rocky Mountain Conference schedule, and on Thursday, January 20, 1927, they boarded the train at the Bozeman station to start a trip to Salt Lake City, where they would face the tall and talented University of Utah Utes. It would be a moment of reckoning for Romney. He was arriving with a team that included his own players from the state, Frank Ward and Cat Thompson, who were as yet untried in the conference. They had gained their individual basketball reputations earlier on the courts in the Beehive State. Frank's brother Orland was developing rapidly but had not yet made the varsity traveling team and was playing on the freshman squad.[153]

On hand at the Deseret Gym to report on the game was the venerable Al Warden, sports editor for the *Ogden Standard-Examiner*, who viewed the well-

85

known Peter Dow of Utah as a powerful force. Warden had written at one time that Dow was a far better basketball player than either Cat or Frank when they were still in Utah and had played in a high school tournament. The Bobcat team was silent on that subject, but they had been stung by Warden's words, and they were looking for revenge. Starting the conference season, the Bobcats were described this time by Warden as "strong and seasoned," even though Ward and Thompson were new to their college team and playing their first conference season.[154]

When the game got underway, the Bobcats appeared at first to be stagestruck, allowing Utah to get an early lead. But they soon gained their composure and quickly caught up with the Utes, punishing them with basket after basket. Most of the scoring came on pivot plays, in which Frank shot it himself or passed off to a cutting forward. In the end, Al Warden had to report honestly on "the northern five winning handily," 47–17. In the victory, Ward and Thompson scored 15 points each. Peter Dow had been the darling of the 1924 high school tournament that had matched the Utah players against each other. This time, the bulky, forceful and clever Dow was smothered by Frank Ward and Brick Breeden, and he managed only a single field goal.[155]

The next night, Saturday, January 22, the Bobcats failed to compete well in the second game against Utah and lost by an embarrassing 37–23 score. Their tired legs from their efforts the first night and suffering from too little sleep showed the Bobcats the importance of disciplined game preparation. Despite the maturity of Frank Ward, Brick Breeden and Cat Thompson, they still had to recognize that the thrill of the victory the night before had left them drained of energy that did not return. Grim-faced, they boarded the train the next morning for a daylong trip back to Bozeman, where they were going to face in-state rival the Montana Grizzlies in two days.

In Bozeman, many MSC Bobcat sports fans thought the only thing that really mattered—blocking out all other achievements—was to beat the rival Montana State University Grizzlies. On January 24, 1927, the Bobcats took the train to Missoula to take on their in-state rival and frequent nemesis, a member of the Pacific Coast Conference and past dominant winners of games against MSC. The rivalry was feisty, with many from Bozeman and Missoula coming to the other town on the train to see the games. There were frequent outbreaks of jeering, and certainly a lot of face-to-face confrontations, triggering temperamental words and shoving and leading to a few cases of fisticuffs. As the Bobcats entered the Grizzlies' gym, the opponents were already on the floor warming up with an aura of cocky confidence that perhaps all their players and fans didn't feel in their hearts. After all—the folks from Missoula would say with well-earned pride—didn't the Grizzlies play in the premier Pacific Coast Athletic Conference in the West against the likes of California, Stanford, Oregon and Washington? Didn't the hayseeds at the "cow college" in Bozeman know that the boys from Missoula were superior in intellect and learning, with their available liberal arts curricula, compared to the boring science, technology, engineering and math taught in Bozeman? Not many at MSC had that kind of confidence; any notions of grandiosity had been beaten out of them in the classroom, where many of the science and engineering professors regularly failed students unless they studied hard and attended all classes. And not many Bobcats cared about poetry. Schubert Dyche did, but then he cared about all things. This day, the Bobcats silenced some of the derision by winning comfortably, 51–32.[156]

The next weekend, Ott Romney's brother Dick brought his Utah State Aggies to Bozeman to face off against the Bobcats in the continuing family rivalry. He lost, 34–29, the first night, and even worse, 40–24, the second. The day after the last Utah State game, BYU came to Bozeman. In games featuring Brick Breeden's defense and the offense of Frank Ward and Cat Thompson, the Cougars lost, 64–37, and, two days later, lost again, 49–33.

A second game that season against the Montana Grizzlies was played in Bozeman. The visitors were beaten soundly, 51–32. Then Carroll College (called Mount Saint Charles at the time) came from Helena to lose, 46–25. Keying off the reliable defense of Brick Breeden, the Bobcat offensive output was slowly increasing, and Romney was starting to see what he wanted from his team.

It was now back on the train to go down to Utah, where the Bobcats beat BYU soundly on their home court in two games, 43–18 and 55–38. A tired Montana State team followed with a loss of the first game to Utah State in Logan, 40–34, followed by a revenge win for the Bobcats the next night, 44–42. On the way home, the Bobcats stopped off in Butte to beat Montana Mines, 50–23, to close out the month of February. In early March, there remained games against Utah, which they won, 47–32 and 50–30, in front of an admiring crowd in Bozeman. With that, the Bobcats had won the Western Division of the Rocky Mountain Conference, and they faced the daunting task of meeting Colorado College, the Eastern Division winner, in a three-game series in Colorado to determine the conference championship.

The Colorado College team was coached by the portly Alvin Twitchell. His strategy was to use a short passing game. It was a style of offense that featured passes that were almost handoffs, and he believed it would confuse the Montana State players. The Bobcat players had practiced defending against that type of game. But despite holding down the Colorado opponents, they lost the first game, 32–31. They came back to win the last two games, and the championship, 29–17 and 32–23.[157] During the playoff series in Colorado, students and fans of the Bobcats back home in Bozeman would gather in the gymnasium, where telegraphed printed reports from the games were rushed up the stairs to the waiting throng. The first thirty copies were in the MSC gym in Bozeman only eight minutes after the buzzer sounded ending the game in Colorado. They gave the jubilant news that the Bobcats had won the Rocky Mountain Championship![158]

The 1927 season was over, and the players could now reflect. Cat Thompson wrote about his first year on the Bobcats: "School was hard my freshman year and I had to work hard just to get average grades. But basketball proved to be a big success for us at Montana State College. We won our conference and most of us were classed as freshmen."[159]

17

MAX WORTHINGTON

And so it is we greatly pride, With honor and esteem—
This man upon whom glory smiles—The Captain of our team.
No knowledge does he lack, Come on fellows put 'er there, Fifteen big ones for Max.
—John McLaughlin, Billings Senior High class of '27 yearbook[160]

At the end of the 1927 season, Ott Romney took a moment to reflect on what had been accomplished. Frank Ward and Cat Thompson had played far above even his lofty expectations, and they were named all-conference, with Ashworth Thompson being named a consensus All-American. Statistics on a national basis were not yet compiled, but as far as anyone could tell, he might have been the leading scorer in the nation. Brick Breeden had played another all-conference season and was the best rim defender in the West and, people were saying, perhaps in the nation. His long arms had swept opponents' misses off the backboard, and sometimes he could rifle the ball down the court to a streaking Cat Thompson or even to Frank Ward, who would be running the length of the floor and moving fast for a big man, showing off the speed he had exhibited in track events.

In the minds of Ott Romney and Schubert Dyche, there was still room for improvement. If the opposing defenses had done their homework, they would know of the scoring ability of Frank and Cat, and sometimes they would attempt to use presses to slow the Bobcat offensive onslaught. It was in overcoming this type of defense that Ott thought he needed even more speed, with the addition of a man who could be a floor guard for the team.

Montana State's Golden Bobcats

The new man would have to work with Brick Breeden in the backcourt to receive his accurate outlet passes after he rebounded the ball and then get the ball down court as fast as possible by dribbling or sending accurate passes to the forwards or the center; and, if he got near the basket, he would have to be capable of scoring. There were other specifics. Ott would like a player who was at least six feet tall and with good hands who never lost the ball. In the back of his mind, Ott kept thinking of Max Worthington of Billings High School as an ideal prospect possessing the attributes he wanted. Max would be graduating from high school, and Ott knew of his reputation and even remembered him from the time he had coached in Billings in 1917. Ott had seen him as a ten-year-old on the playgrounds, and his athletic ability caught everyone's eye.

Max grew up in Billings as the most athletic member of his family, which included an older brother, LaSelle Worthington, named for his mother. Her maiden name was Mary LaSelle. She had married Leonard L. Worthington, who went by the nickname "Len"; some would say it was "Lon" he liked to be called.[161] The site of their wedding was Beatrice, Nebraska, on November 16, 1905, at her parents' home. The ceremony was performed by a local minister. Soon after that, the couple moved to Billings, where Mary became a Christian Scientist who practiced and adhered to the religion. Max's bruises and cuts suffered on the crude playgrounds did not get him to the doctor. He just had to let things heal and be tough, and he was.[162]

Max had all kinds of talent as a boy, and he turned heads on the playgrounds. In school races and jumps, he excelled, and in playground basketball, his shots went in. On the rock-strewn neighborhood gridirons, he ran through defenders and threw and caught passes—bloody knees and elbows were ignored. When Billings High School hired Ott Romney as its coach in 1917, Lon would take young Max to Ott's football practices and then to his basketball practices to observe the discipline the coach was instilling in the older boys. Max could hardly wait until it was his time to play for the charismatic coach. But this goal was something Max could not utter even as a young boy, because the discipline in the Worthington house called for modesty of words. Performance was the only measure of a man's success, and self-glorification was never allowed.[163]

By 1925, Max had become the star high school player he had hoped to be, but he missed out on his dream of playing for Ott Romney, who had left Billings after the 1918 season. A few years later, the Worthington household awoke to headlines that Ott was coming back to Montana, this time as head

1929 Basketball National Champions

Left: Max Worthington as a football player in high school. *Courtesy Billings Public Library collections. Digital Collection, Billings Public Library. Billings, Montana, Yellowstone County, Montana.*

Right: Max Worthington, captain of the 1927 Billings High School football team. Kyote, *1927 Billings High School Yearbook. Digital Collection, Billings Public Library. Billings, Montana; Yellowstone County, Montana.*

coach at Montana State College. As young Max leaned back in his chair at the breakfast table and read the article, a look of purpose crossed his face, enough for Lon to ask him his thoughts. "I want to go to Montana State and play for coach Romney," Max said shortly. "You mean that?" Lon asked, and when Max nodded, Lon told him he had better get up early and practice every day, because that man would not have him on his team unless he did. "I know," Max said, picking up his sports bag and heading out the door.[164]

In 1925, with Max playing, Billings High had a fine basketball team that went to the National High School Tournament sponsored by the University of Chicago and its legendary coach, Amos Alonzo Stagg. They played their first game against ultimate tournament champion Fitchburg Academy from Massachusetts, which had to figure out a defense against

Montana State's Golden Bobcats

The Billings High School team playing a 1927 basketball game against Helena before a packed crowd in the Montana State gymnasium. Kyote, *1927 Billings High School yearbook*. *Montana State University*.

Max in the second half to pull out a 33–20 victory. The next morning, the Billings team defeated Hagerstown, the champions of Maryland, 32–26, but then they lost the day after, 33–25, to a team from, of all places, Salt Lake City. In its three games in the tournament, the Billings team was narrowly outscored, 84–77.[165]

It was the Montana state high school basketball tournament in 1927 that made Ott Romney focus principally on Max, who had received the Bobcat Award, given every year at the end of the tournament to the player who best added aggressiveness, sportsmanship and value to his team. Ott Romney decided to actively seek him out to become the fifth starter on the Golden Bobcats.[166]

When Ott decided it was time to inquire seriously about Max, he was told that the word from the Worthington family was that Max and his friend and former teammate Clyde Carpenter were planning to enroll together at the university in Missoula and would be playing for the Grizzlies. Then a miracle happened. Max and Clyde were traveling to Missoula when the train broke down a short distance from Bozeman. Repairs were made, but about eight hours had passed, making the remaining hours of the trip required to get to Missoula seem like an eternity. As the train's brakes started squealing for a stop in Bozeman, Max reconsidered his college decision. He knew he didn't want to be any farther away from home than the 140 miles from there to

Billings. Getting off the train in north Bozeman, Max walked all the way to the Sigma Alpha Epsilon fraternity house, where his brother LaSelle was a member and who could direct him to Ott Romney to tell him he would like to play for the Bobcats.[167]

 Later on, Max felt compelled to pledge his brother's fraternity, even though by then he knew of Romney's preference for Sigma Chi. But it didn't make any difference, because a man of Romney's character was not about to play favorites. Fraternal brotherhood was one thing, but winning was overriding. By God, Ott would win even if he had to rely on an SAE!

18

1927–28 SEASON

Putting the Championship Team Together

The men who have made the Bobcat squad of 1927–1928 are: Capt. John "Brick" Breeden all-conference guard of Bozeman. Breeden has been called Montana's greatest basketball guard of all time….Ashworth "Cat" Thompson all-conference forward of La Verkin, Utah. Thompson is the spectacular player of the school and of the conference, being high scorer of the conference last season…he is the hardest man in the conference to guard. Frank Ward, center, of Parowan, Utah. Chosen center on many all-conference and all-division outfits last year.
—Billings Gazette, *December 15, 1927*

In the fall of 1927, the preseason outlook was rosy for the Montana State Bobcat basketball team. Ott Romney felt satisfaction in having Max Worthington on the team, but this was just part of the equation. The papers were raving about the play the previous year of Cat Thompson, captain Brick Breeden and Frank Ward, and all three were back.[168]

Max Worthington told his own story about how he became a starter as a freshman just out of high school.

[In 1927,] *Ott Romney, who was the director of athletics and coach of everything in those days, came to Billings…and invited me to come to MSC. He said he could give me some help. At that particular time help was of interest because banks had failed. So things were pretty tight in terms of financing. So I* [came to MSC] *and started in agriculture, and played freshman football. Then came basketball, and that's what Romney wanted*

1929 Basketball National Champions

The 1927 Bobcat team. Coach Ott Romney is at upper left, and Assistant Coach Schubert Dyche is at upper right. *1927* Montanan.

> *me for. Frank Worden, from Butte and I were competing for the guard job that opened as the result of the graduation of Val Glynn. Worden was a fine athlete....We...split the time for a while, and then all of a sudden I was the one getting the start as a freshman.*[169]

Tragically, Frank Worden died the next year.

In the fall of 1927, Ott Romney looked over the schedule he had arranged and thought without hesitation—and certainly without modesty—that he would win all the games. Still, it depended on the players themselves.

Cat Thompson usually stayed after practice to shoot and dribble late at night, and Max Worthington stayed with him to learn. The *Helena Independent Record* said of Thompson, "The Dixie Flyer is five feet and nine inches tall and one of the finest physical specimens in Montana State College. He has never smoked or touched liquor, trains carefully through the entire year."[170]

The social life at the Montana State fraternities was in full bloom, and with the Mormons involved, it undoubtedly created conflicts. Ott Romney was the fraternity advisor of Sigma Chi, and a blind eye was possibly turned to fraternity parties, even though he was known to be a rigid adherent to the sober principles of his faith. Cat Thompson and Orland Ward were steadfast in their absolute refusal to break training. If this created problems, they ended soon when Max Worthington, a member of the rival SAE fraternity, supplied the glue that kept the team together. A deadly serious adherent to training and discipline, he wanted nothing to get in the way of peak athletic performances, and his example solidified the team's commitment to rigorous training.[171] The Bobcats opened their 1927–28 season in the traditional way, taking on the Livingston Railway club team. This year, the Railroaders were not up to their usual level of play and lost, 77–7 and 103–15. With the bench players wanting to score, it was difficult for the Bobcats to keep the score down. They then won easily, 36–17, over the Montana School of Mines in what for the Bobcats was a low-production game against a lesser team.[172]

The University of Idaho came to Bozeman the next week for a three-game series. The first game was a lopsided victory for the Bobcats, 57–28. However, Romney witnessed a disappointment the next night on December 23, when the roles were reversed and the Idaho team played a precision game against the suddenly erratic Bobcat five that gave them a 46–41 victory.[173] Idaho did it with a short passing game, which the Bobcats had faced before, but this time they could not defend against it without fouling. A Vandal would start to shoot, and the quicker Bobcats would close on him right away, only to have the shooter shovel the ball off—almost a football handoff—to a teammate cutting by who would in turn hand it off to another, more open teammate nearby. The Bobcats could only grab and foul the Idaho players to prevent them from moving the ball this way. Rallying from a big halftime deficit, the Bobcats kept a win in sight until the Vandals froze the ball in the last minutes to protect their lead. An angry Frank Ward tried to take matters into his own hands, but it was too late, despite the fact that he had dominated at center with 16 points on seven field goals. Thompson had 11 points on four field goals, but it was not enough, and the Vandals gave them a loss, 46–41.

On the third night, the Bobcats got a small lead and held on, 45–44. The game could have easily gone the other way; if it had, losing two games to the same team on their own home court would have disgraced the Bobcats, but disaster was avoided. Downtown in Bozeman, some of the loyal fans were grumbling, and some were even predicting a total collapse for the season.[174]

Since the Vandals were out in the Wild West, maybe it was fitting that gunfire ended the last game—or so the fans thought. A track meet starter's pistol was used in those days to signal the end of a game, and fans were sitting close behind the timekeeper, who had the gun. "When the game ended that official, instead of firing his pistol in the air, he poked it in back of him between the chairs and pulled the trigger. So near was the muzzle to a man's foot that the wadding cut the flesh like a bullet would, and the flash of powder set his sock on fire."[175]

After the Idaho games, Romney sat with furrowed brow, thinking of what could be done to perfect a defensive scheme that would stop the troublesome short passing games used against them. He consulted Schubert, and they developed a tight 2-3 zone, packed in under the basket, with careful attention given to his players moving into defensive position early on any open man cutting for a handoff. That would have to be perfected on the road, because the Bobcats had to depart on a long trip to Colorado to play both college and well-known club teams.

Getting to Colorado from Bozeman was not easy. Driving wasn't acceptable, because the trip was about eight hundred miles one-way on dirt roads. Two train routes were available to get to Denver. One was through Ogden and then east to Denver. The alternative was to use the GB&Q Railway Company, which had given a good rate to the Bobcats for team travel south out of Billings.[176] Montana State chose the route through Billings, and there was time for them to play a game or two on the way. That resulted in a doubleheader in the Billlings High School gym, where they would be playing the Hardin Moose club team in the first game and Beherent's Billings All-Stars club in the second game.

Ott was always looking for opportunities to play his reserves, but the philosophy of the day emphasized having the starters on the floor as long as possible to take advantage of their teamwork. The trick was to pick the right starters. Romney adhered to this philosophy, but he still thought he had talent on his bench. So, in the Hardin Moose game, just his bench played. They scored only three field goals, the same number as the opponent. The final score was an embarrassing 10–8 win.

With the first game of the doubleheader over, the Billings fans finally welcomed the true first-team Bobcats to the floor to play the Beherent's club team. Ott Romney knew the affection Billings had for Max Worthington and Peck McFarland, and they received standing ovations. When Ott put them in the game with the green light to shoot, they put up impressive numbers, with Peck ending with nine field goals and 20 points and Max with seven field goals and 15 points to give the fans what they were looking for from the locals. The score was 93–38.[177]

With the Billings exhibition games out of the way, the Bobcats boarded the train for the trip through Wyoming to Denver, a long distance on a swaying railroad car in which the rhythmic beat of the wheels on the tracks was sleep-robbing to some. But to the tired Bobcats, it was the only rest they would get. Their first game was in Denver against the University of Denver Pioneers, a Rocky Mountain Conference Eastern Division team. Despite their history as one of the oldest basketball programs in the country, they were no match for the speedy Bobcats, who won the game, 57–34.[178]

The next day, the Bobcats made their way to Greely to take on the Colorado State Teachers, another member of the Rocky Mountain Conference. Frank Ward came out shooting and early on had 13 points, and when he slowed down in the second half, Cat Thompson took over with 10 points. The final score was 43–27 in a game that was played remarkably fast by the Teachers, but their speed was matched.[179] The next night, the Bobcats continued their "victorious march through Colorado," as the Associated Press called it. They won, 40–31, in a game in which they took a commanding lead in the first half, which ended 21–13. The Teachers weren't dead yet and wouldn't roll over, fighting back to a 29–27 deficit until the erratic Peck McFarland, whose legs were fresh, came off the bench and scored eight field goals to win the game, marking one of the very few times Romney's bench was that reliable.[180] Before leaving Colorado, the tired Bobcats won on New Year's Eve, 48–42, against the experienced Denver area players of the AAU Pratt's Bookstore team.

Romney still wanted more nonconference games. He believed strongly that the more a team played, the stronger the players got, and he did not believe in long periods of rest. He wanted the team to be ready at all times, under any condition, to play with all their ability. On New Year's Day, the Bobcats started traveling through Wyoming on the way home to Bozeman. Romney had arranged a game against the All-Stars of Sheridan, Wyoming, which was on the route. On January 2, 1928, the Bobcats easily won, 51–13.[181]

In Romney's mind, the exhibition games and the Colorado trip had been a success, because it had given him a better handle on his personnel. If for no other reason, the trip had been successful because he had repaired the defense, which could now stop short-passing offenses, which had been a problem for him.

The Bobcats were home only one day before they had to take on the barnstorming Haymakers from Phillips University of Enid, Oklahoma, a school founded in 1907 by the Disciples of Christ denomination. The

Haymakers played in the tough Oklahoma State Conference and had been runners-up in the 1927 national AAU tournament. They struck fear in the hearts of their opponents. It turned out the Bobcats were more than ready for them, and the Haymakers played well only during the first ten minutes. At that point, Cat Thompson, who had been held out in an experiment, came into the game from the bench and started the MSC scoring. It was finished in the second half by Max Worthington, whom Romney was trying out at a forward position, where he got more shots than he usually did at guard. The Haymakers went down, 48–22, in the first game and 38–31 in the second, but it was the first game that was so instructional. Wanting to give Cat Thompson a rest, Romney had started the unpredictable Peck McFarland opposite Max at forward for the Bobcats, but he had only 5 points. Breeden was, as usual, the defensive force on the team, and while scoring only 1 point, he ripped off many rebounds, and his long and accurate outlet passes started the offense for his fast-breaking teammates.[182]

The highlight of the early-season home games was the appearance, just two days after the Haymakers game, of the Oregon State Beavers. They had come a long way by train from Salem to take on the Bobcats, who people were now calling the premier team in the West. Not many teams wanted to venture into Bozeman, which their coaches viewed as dangerously inaccessible and required a long, fatiguing train ride. The Beavers were one of the few teams that had come to the Bobcat den and tangled with their tree "Cat," John Ashworth Thompson. They played bravely, only to leave in disappointment after losing, 56–36. A moral victory of sorts was that the Oregon team was trailing by only six points in a slow-starting first half. The Beavers opened the game with a series of trick plays that caught the Bobcats by surprise. Ott Romney was going to have nothing to do with their deceptions in the second half and put his team in a man-to-man defense that stopped the passing of the Beavers and caused them to turn over the ball when they tried anything fancy.[183]

A few days later, the Bobcats themselves boarded a train and headed west to Pullman to take on the Cougars of Washington State University. While the WSU fans expected a victory, they soon found that they had underestimated Montana State, which was simply too fast. Still, in the recent memory of the fans were the exploits of the 1917 Cougars, who, as a wonder team of the decade, had won the national championship under coach Bohler. Now, in 1928, they were gathered in the brand-new gymnasium that they had waited patiently for since construction started in 1925. The fans expected top-flight basketball—and wins. Neither the new gym nor the reputation of WSU's

Brick Breeden. *Courtesy Montana State University Special Collections Photo Archives.*

vaunted coach impressed the Bobcats, who led 32–12 at the half. The final score was 58–31, as the Bobcats inched closer to Romney's prediction of 60 points per game.[184]

There was still another game against Washington State the next night, and Ott Romney's worst fears came true. He had always worried that the success of the Bobcats would go to their heads and that they would become overconfident. He had cautioned them not to get cocky. The Bobcats had an early lead before they almost fell into the trap they had set for themselves. Brick Breeden was suffering from a sprained ankle from the first game, and Romney had failed to make the changes that would have moderated his absence. Washington State came on with consistent passing, leading to point production that kept the Cougars within rallying distance through most of the game. It was left up to Cat Thompson, who scored a record fourteen field goals on his way to 29 points to beat the Cougars almost single-handedly. He had three baskets in less than forty seconds without a miss. In the end, after a scare, the Bobcats won handily, 57–42.[185]

Back in Bozeman, on January 16, 1928, the Bobcats took on their in-state rival and frequent nemesis, the Montana State University Grizzlies. At the opening tip, Frank Ward tapped the ball to Cat Thompson, who passed back to Max Worthington and then broke for the basket before the Grizzlies were even set. Receiving in stride a perfect pass from Max, Cat scored the first basket. He ended up scoring as many points, 26, as the Grizzly team did for the game, and Frank Ward was only a free throw behind him with 25. Max Worthington played a great floor game while scoring 11. The Bobcats were unstoppable and totaled an amazing 76 points to an embarrassing 26 for the Grizzlies.

It was now time for Ott Romney and Schubert Dyche to start preparing the team to travel south to Utah to start the conference season. Ott had scheduled a warm-up game with the team from Montana Normal School, the teacher's college in Dillon, a railway town of about two thousand just over the Monida Pass from Idaho. The Bobcats won easily, 81–23.[186]

The set shooting by the team had become a thing of great pride. In those days, set shots were typically taken with both feet flat on the floor, the front leg on the side of the shooting hand planted about half a stride in front of the back leg. The body was then dipped, and the ball was launched with a push shot, either with one hand for those who could maintain ball control or two hands if they could not. Sometimes, the ball was even shot underhanded, but this took time and space to get the shot off. Another version of the set shot was to raise the knee on the side of the shooting hand for establishing balance and leaning the body toward the basket while letting the ball go.

Cat Thompson had another style for performing set shots, one that would eventually be adopted by other players. He had large hands and could easily maintain ball control, and he had perfect body balance. He soon developed a set shot that put all his weight on the leg on the same side as his shooting hand. His body would be in an erect posture on the ball of his shooting side foot, and when he got off his shot, his offside leg would be moving forward to give him balance. To the crowd in the Montana State gymnasium, this appeared to be somewhat awkward, but shot after shot rippled through the cords of the net. As the season wore on, the fans began to appreciate Cat's shots as things of beauty. He could get them off so quickly that few opponents had time to attempt a block. If opponents started crowding, Cat could easily put the ball on the floor to get around them on his way to the basket.[187]

19

THE 1928 CONFERENCE SEASON

Repeating their performance of last year and adding new laurels the Bobcat wonder team swept to another Conference Championship in dazzling manner when they took Wyoming University, champions of the Eastern Division to camp every game of the Championship Series which was held at Bozeman.
—*1928* Montanan

The intensity of the Rocky Mountain Conference almost caught the Bobcats emotionally unprepared as they approached their first conference encounter of the 1928 season. Down in Utah, Les Goates, a young sports reporter with flowery writing, was subbing for Al Warden at the *Ogden Standard-Examiner*. Early on, just before the Bobcats were about to meet BYU in Provo, he showed disdain for the Montanans. It was something he would regret, because a month later, he had to admit that the Bobcats were on a path to win the conference. The cynical reporter and the rest of the basketball fans in Utah had to recognize that the Bobcats won eighteen of their nineteen games already that season and were on a roll to defeat anyone they played.[188] Sure enough, the Bobcats, even when not playing up to their standard, beat BYU, 43–41, on Friday night and 43–37 on Saturday night. It was the distance shooting of Cat Thompson and the Ward brothers that did it. The game had not been without problems, as, unexpectedly, the BYU team came out with a fast passing attack that bewildered the seemingly tired Bobcats. They would chase after the ball, only to see the Cougars hit an open man for a basket. If it hadn't been for Cat Thompson's shooting, the Bobcats might have lost.[189]

1929 Basketball National Champions

"The Squad." Ott Romney (*upper left*), Schubert Dyche (*upper right*), Frank Ward (*third from left, upper row*), Brick Breeden (*fouth from left, upper row*), Max Worthington (*next to Schubert Dyche*), Orland Ward (*third from left, front row*), Cat Thompson (*fourth from left*). *1928* Montanan.

The team returned home Sunday, and Ott Romney needed to give them at least a day's rest. But he couldn't do that, because they had to play the next night in Missoula against the Montana Grizzlies, who had lost their first game, 76–26. But that game was in Bozeman. This time, the Grizzlies were tougher. But they weren't tough enough even for the tired Bobcats, and they were beaten at home, 52–39.

Afterward, a game against the Butte YMCA netted a 68–34 win, but it almost spelled disaster when Thompson sprained his ankle.[190] He healed up quickly, in time for the upcoming games in Bozeman. They were against the Utah schools, which were attracting sellout crowds, with a thousand visiting high school students also expected in attendance. Extra seats were again being put in to swell the capacity of the elegant MSC gym.

On Monday night, January 30, Montana State College opened its home-game defense of the Rocky Mountain Conference title against the Utah Aggies. The Bobcats erased a lead held by the visitors in the first half and then got a lead that was held throughout the second half before the biggest basketball crowds ever seen in Bozeman. The attendance was standing-room only, in fact. The Aggies were beaten, 57–39. Frank Ward, playing against Utah State's outstanding center Glen Worthington (no relation to

Brick Breeden was the captain of the 1928 Bobcats. *1928* Montanan.

Max), scored 20 points and was the sensation of the battle of the top players. It was a bitter defeat for Ott's brother Dick, the Aggie coach, who had hoped the Bobcats would continue their slump. Again, older brother Ott held the upper hand.

The second game was sure to be a hard-fought, rough, physical contest between two teams, with their powerful centers and shooters muscling their way into position against one another. When Tuesday night came, the Bobcats were ready for the conflict and confident that they could wear down the Aggies, but they had to consider the fact that Frank Ward was both hobbled and sick. In what became Utah State's first conference win of the year, 47–44, the Aggies got physical with the Bobcats in an attempt to beat them at their own game. Frank was not himself and took punishment underneath the boards time after time as Aggie center Glenn Worthington poured in shots over and around him to lead both teams with ten field goals.[191]

Finally, an injured Frank Ward had to leave the game. He could only look on in glowering frustration and vow revenge. As the game proceeded, it became apparent that the Bobcats would lose unless a miracle happened— and it almost did. Cat Thompson refused to give up and kept the offensive pressure on the visitors in a way that only he could. A paper reported: "It was a dramatic basketball game in spots, rough as a Kansas tornado, and climactic near the end when 'Cat' Thompson, Montana's great little forward turned loose a spurt of baskets that drew his team within one point of the victory." The Bobcats actually were 3 points from the victory, 47–43, at the end. Thompson finished the game with nine field goals and drew fouls on his acrobatic drives to the basket that gave him seven free throws.[192]

"Cat" Thompson. *1928 Montanan.*

The one loss to Utah State on the home court had a traumatizing affect among the Bozeman boosters. Some of the naysayers thought the Bobcats were finished for the season. By way of contrast, almost never had Cat Thompson played better. But the gloom persisted around Montana, with fans being reminded by the midweek paper that even Jack Dempsey, who had once defended his heavyweight title in Shelby, Montana, against Tommy Gibbons had to give up the fight game.[193]

By Friday night, February 3, things had started to look better for the Bobcats. In what was described as a colorless game, they defeated the University of Utah Utes in Bozeman, 46–38. Despite winning, the Bobcats were simply off, and observers said they were listless and woefully weak. If it hadn't been for Orland Ward rising to the occasion with 17 points, the game might have been a loss. But the victory gave the Bobcats four wins in the conference against the one defeat to their biggest rival that year, the Utah State Aggies, who were now tied with Utah in second place.[194]

On February 4, the Bobcats again played Utah, and the Montana papers said they were in their worst form in two years. "Woefully poor," the *Helena Independent* said of the shooting. What was worse, Cat Thompson got into a scuffle with a bigger Utah guard, who threw him to the floor, causing a hip injury. Grimacing in pain, Thompson stayed in the game. He finished almost on one foot and did not suit up for practices the next week. Max Worthington stepped in and was the spirit that moved the Bobcats to victory, 33–22. He was playing splendidly on defense and scored 10 points to add to Thompson's 11. Frank Ward scored only one basket and two free throws in a miserable game for him, in which he allowed Smith, the Utah center, to score 12 points. Embarrassed, he silently vowed it would never happen again.[195]

Ott commented publicly on the lifeless victories and stated that the "whirlwind" forward, Thompson, would lead the Bobcats back to their old speed in scoring.[196] No one was really sure that Cat would be up to it, because he was still limping; but, there was no time off and they had to quickly play Carroll College of Helena and Montana Mines of Butte, on successive nights in games they won, 61–43 and 39–19.

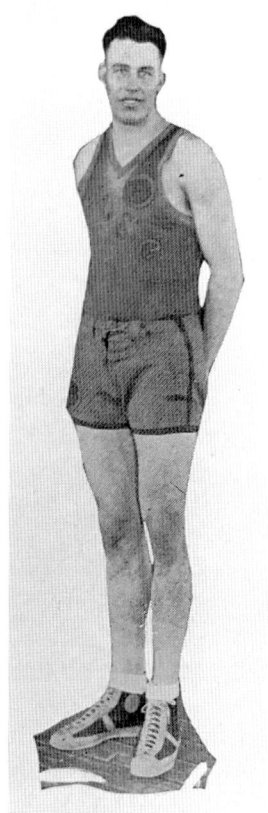

Frank Ward. *1928* Montanan.

Orland Ward got a break when his competition for playing time, Gilbert "Peck" McFarland, went missing just when the team was going to travel to Utah. His absence wasn't missed for long, because it resulted in Orland developing rapidity as a player once he got the additional time that had been given to Peck.[197]

By the time they left Butte, the Montana papers were hailing the Bobcats as the "wonder team." They already had a record of seventeen wins in eighteen games; never before had a Rocky Mountain Conference team started with such an impressive record. Not counting their wins against independent teams, the Bobcats had averaged 50.4 points a game against their college competition. In those games, Cat Thompson was averaging 16.2 points per game, and Frank Ward was at 13.9 points with many rebounds.[198]

The team suffered what could have been a disaster on the way down to Utah. To save time and money, Ott Romney had decided that immediately after the game in Butte they would drive down in their own cars to Utah. The car that Max Worthington was riding in got stuck on Monida Pass in a snowdrift, and Max's feet became frozen when he helped shovel the car out. He lost his toenails. But when the Bobcats took the floor against Utah State, Max hobbled on.

Orland Ward. *1928* Montanan.

The team was ready for its first game in Logan against Utah State, and the newspaper reported, "Monday night, the Bobcats were plainly masters of the game." They scored early and got a lead that was never relinquished. It was the 20-point scoring of Thompson that put the Bobcats out of reach, aided by 23 points between the Ward brothers and a stellar defensive game by Brick Breeden. Max Worthington fought through his injury and played long enough and well enough to score a solid 9 points.[199] The final score was 55–42.

The Bobcats rested in Logan on Tuesday; on Wednesday night, they played the Aggies again. Utah State trailed 12–18 at halftime, but they opened the second half with some scoring and tied the game, 30–30. It was reported: "From then on until the finish the two teams battled evenly until baskets by Ward and Thompson in the closing minutes of play iced the game for the visitors." The final score was 39–35, with Frank Ward leading the Bobcats with 16 points.[200]

Friday night found the Bobcats in Salt Lake City to play Utah. Coming out of the hotel across the street from Deseret Gym, Frank Ward decided it was time to even some old scores. He had played well there in 1926 as a member of the BAC junior-college team, but he had received little interest from the University of Utah to join its squad, and he wanted to show them how wrong they were in not recruiting him. Despite Frank scoring only 10 points, the Bobcats hung on for a 44–39 victory, but the result could have been different without the good shooting of Orland Ward, who bailed out his brother by scoring 16 points despite being in foul trouble.[201] The next night, both teams were sluggish from their first game and off the mark with their shots. The Bobcats staggered to a 27–22 victory.

Then the Bobcats drove back up over the mountains to Montana, where they had almost a full week of rest. They played in Bozeman on March 1 against the visiting BYU Cougars, who had been beaten by the Bobcats twice on their home court in the middle of January. The Cougars were bent on revenge, but they did not have enough firepower to come close, and they were beaten, 69–44, and again the next night, 57–41. With these victories, the Bobcats won the Western Division and were now ready to move on to the Rocky Mountain Conference championship, to be played in Bozeman.[202]

Wyoming was the champion of the Eastern Division, and they came to town as though they were favorites to win. Coach Stewart Park and his team got off the train in Bozeman at noon on Sunday, ready for the opening the next night of their three-game series. The Cowboys appeared in good condition, with two of their players who had been ill now fully recovered. They took advantage of the Sunday afternoon break in Bozeman to go to the gymnasium, where they donned their workout uniforms and went through a spirited scrimmage. On Monday, they returned early for warm-ups to get ready for the game they seemed confident they would win.

As to the probable outcome of the three-game series, those who knew Romney knew that he believed the Bobcats could take the Wyoming squad easily. When Wyoming's coach was questioned by a reporter from the *Bozeman Daily Chronicle*, he said: "We will have no alibi if we lose. Wyoming will play the kind of ball that won her the division championship. We know the Bobcats are strong and expect a hard struggle."

As the drama was about to unfold, MSC officials announced that all reserved seats for the game were sold out, but they were rolling in about one thousand temporary seats for those coming at the last minute. At game time, the gym was overflowing, and the roar of the crowd was deafening as the Bobcats entered the arena in their home gold uniforms with blue trim.[203]

In the first game, both teams started slowly. During the season, the Wyoming team had averaged far fewer points, and their strategy was to hold the ball as long as they could to keep it away from the high-scoring Bobcats. The first few Cowboy shots fell, and they even had the lead early on, but it would not be held for long. Awakened, the Bobcats huddled to plan their attack, which was to fast-break from the bad shots the Cowboys started to take. It worked, and Montana State started to score. As the Cowboys became frustrated and put up even worse shots, the Bobcats grabbed more

1929 Basketball National Champions

rebounds and raced down the court to put the ball in the basket. They won the game, 43–27.

The series was scheduled for three games. Having won the first game, the Bobcats did not want to risk letting the Wyoming team squeak out a win in the second game to tie the series. Remembering that the slow play of Wyoming had put the Cowboys in the lead the previous night, the Bobcats went to their uptempo game right away and began a dazzling attack that bewildered their opponent's players, who could only watch as the Bobcat team sprinted past them to score easy layups. Cat Thompson set the single-game scoring record for a conference title game, and the paper said that "Montana's 'blonde dynamo' scored 28 points…against Wyoming's tall guards almost at will, as his quick footwork got him open time and again." Nearly doubling the score, the Bobcats coasted to

The 1952 reunion of the Golden Bobcats, held at Montana State College on the occasion of Ott Romney receiving an honorary doctorate from MSU and the naming of the gymnasium after him. Shown are Schubert Dyche (*front row, second from left*) and Ott Romney (*front row, third from left*) and some members of the Golden Bobcat team. *Courtesy Montana State University Library Special Collections.*

the win, 59–31. With that, they won the Rocky Mountain Conference championship a second time in as many years.

Since a third game had been scheduled in the best-of-three series, it was played, even though the Bobcats had already clinched the title. This time, Wyoming gathered its composure and played up to their ability, even leading the game for a time. But the resourceful Bobcats put on one of their fighting finishes to win, 43–36.[204]

At the end of the 1928 season, the newspapers around the country carried an article and sketches of ten outstanding collegiate basketball players constituting the consensus All-American team. The players were from Pennsylvania, Oklahoma, Southern California, Pittsburgh, Mississippi, Arkansas and Indiana. It was the inclusion of Cat Thompson with the group for the second year in a row that brought joy to the hearts of the loyal Bobcat fans in the mountains of Montana.[205]

Emboldened by the successful season, Romney sent out challenges to powerful eastern and western schools outside the Rocky Mountains. He offered to take the Bobcats on the road for the games, but the schools either refused or did not respond. With no takers, the season ended, and the players turned in their uniforms.[206] [207]

20

OTT ROMNEY LEAVES HIS TEAM AFTER THE 1928 SEASON

Every man who wore a Blue and Gold suit emblematic of the basketball squad will return again next year but the man who put the fight into them and developed the man to man defense and five man offense, G. Ott Romney, will be leading one of our chief competitors, B.Y.U., and we wish him luck as he leaves Montana State College after leading our athletic destinies for eight years.
—*1928* Montanan[208] [209]

March roared into Bozeman in the spring of 1928 with its usual blustery, cold and unpredictable weather. Snowstorms turned to blizzards in one day, then brief, melting sunshine appeared the next, but only for a few hours. High winds then followed, then rain, sleet and angry swirling gray clouds giving no comfort to those who were looking for the end of winter. But there was another storm on the horizon, unrelated to the weather. As early as March 17, the papers were reporting that Ott Romney might be considering coaching offers from either Utah or BYU. There was also a rumor that he would be on a year's leave of absence.[210] His leaving had been whispered about for a while, so it wasn't a total surprise in Bozeman. It had gotten out as early as the previous December that a man named John McGough had already been hired as Bobcat coach.

There was something strange about all this. McGough's hiring had been announced by the Greater University of Montana, the state's higher education authority, which oversaw both the Bozeman and Missoula campuses. It was a move outside the state chancellor's jurisdiction and would never be accepted by MSC president Alfred Atkinson when he got back from a leave of absence, which he had been on at the time.[211] [212]

The papers in Utah predicted outright that Romney would be going to BYU and would be offered a "fat" contract.[213] On March 24, 1928, the *Ogden Standard-Examiner* confirmed that George Ottinger Romney was leaving Montana State for Brigham Young University, where he would be athletic director and head coach. Making matters appear even worse was the announcement that Schubert Dyche, the athletic trainer at MSC, would be coming along with Ott. The announcement made all the rumors a reality, and this time, it hit the town of Bozeman like a sledgehammer. The players, having just won the Rocky Mountain Conference title and completing a season that saw two of their teammates named national All-Americans, were mystified. Hadn't Ott told them he would be with them to the end of their college days, particularly the Utah players who had come to play for him? The Ward brothers and Cat Thompson were hit particularly hard. As Utah Mormons, there had been a time in each of their lives when they would have preferred to play for BYU, which had shown no interest. And to think, Ott Romney was going to be the coach of that team.[214]

If Schubert Dyche did not go with Ott Romney, there was some support for him to be elevated to head coach of the Bobcats. Then again, some people didn't think he could handle the job. Didn't the team deserve a coach better than a clarinet player in the orchestra? Schubert was also known to be just a little on the odd side, shy and reticent and easily distracted by whatever was on his mind at the moment. He had done things like shutting the lights off in the office he shared, leaving his office mate working in the dark. He was not comfortable at all when he had to address the local boosters, and his talks in team huddles were not so much pep talks as careful instructions to mature players who generated their own passion. In the end, though, the majority of the boosters supported him, recognizing his quiet competence.[215]

Fanning the flames of the movement to keep Schubert Dyche were the rumors that the entire starting team might leave Montana State if both coaches left. The stories had it

Ott Romney. *Courtesy Montana State University Special Collections Photo Archives.*

1929 Basketball National Champions

Schubert Dyche (*left*) replaced Ott Romney as the new MSC coach starting in the fall of 1928. *Courtesy Montana State University Special Collections Photo Archives.*

that the Bobcats would form an AAU team and be paid to play by one of the many companies in the country that wanted to sponsor basketball's best. They would look to field a team like the Cook Painters out of Kansas City, who were making a national name for themselves and their sponsor, the Cook Paint Company. It was the highest level of basketball competition of the time and an attractive proposition to the Bobcat players, given their ages. It was particularly enticing for Frank Ward, who had a family to take care of.

Until that time, Schubert Dyche had faced another obstacle. He had never been in line for a head coaching job, because he had never finished his college education. He started college back in Colorado but had to quit, mostly because he was out of funds and couldn't afford it.[216] He had been given quite a bit of college credit from courses taken in the summertime at several schools but had never accumulated enough to graduate. Unless corrected, this could disqualify him for the job.

No one was giving any thought to Schubert's personal life, which was a disaster. The previous summer session, he had returned to Utah, planning to take coursework toward a possible degree in botany and bacteriology at Utah State in Logan. But that didn't work out, because he had other things on his mind. He had been seeing June Shepherd, a young lady in Salt Lake City who excelled as an athlete in swimming, diving and baseball.[217] [218] On June 13, 1927, Schubert Dyche, thirty-four, and June Shepherd, nineteen, were married. They returned to make their home in Bozeman, where they stayed for but a few days before they took summer jobs with the city recreation department in Havre, Montana. It was perfect for the athletic pair, with June supervising girls and Schubert leading the boys in programs that included swimming and baseball. At the end of the summer, they were back in Bozeman, and Schube resumed his duties as Romney's assistant.[219]

June Dyche was not enthusiastic about the idea of her husband going to Utah with Romney. The papers reported that she was not Mormon, and even though she had been raised in Salt Lake City, they thought she would have trouble fitting in at Provo. There was another reason. June was expecting their first child soon. Without going into all of his reasons, Schubert finally let it be known that he would have difficulty moving to Provo and would consider staying at MSC if he had the support of the community. More than seventy prominent boosters in and around Bozeman submitted a petition urging MSC to keep Schubert Dyche. So confident did this make him that he was emboldened to take the negotiating position that if he were not made coach and athletic director he would rather go to BYU with Romney. For a couple of years, his modesty and reticence had kept him quiet on one important subject, but now he let it be known that he was the one most responsible for getting Cat Thompson and the Ward brothers to MSC. Many may have assumed that this was due to the magnetism of Ott Romney.[220]

MSC professor Deane Swingle was assigned by President Atkinson to put together a proposal aimed at keeping Dyche as coach. It was an uphill task. As Swingle said, "First…he lacks stage presence and second, that he is highly sensitive to critics." Swingle was quick to note that these faults were probably less significant than faults that might be found in the as-yet-unknown coaches from outside the college who might be applying for the job. It was also Swingle's fear that if Dyche were lost, there might be financial extravagances, something he considered Romney's weakness, and they might lose the wholesome influence that Dyche gave to Montana State. When Swingle finished his report, he gave his recommendation that Dyche be offered the job.[221] Soon, it was formally announced that Dyche would receive his bachelor of science degree from MSC and was being appointed professor of physical education and director of athletics, succeeding Ott Romney.[222] Shube had gotten what he wanted.

All of the turmoil had its toll on June. She was in the last term of her pregnancy during the indecision about her husband's job. Outwardly, she was doing fine. She was healthy and only twenty years old at the time, fourteen years younger than her husband. June went into labor and was taken to the hospital, where she gave birth to a healthy baby boy. Tragically, she died in the operating room. Other than naming the little boy Schubert June Dyche, to honor his wife, Shube knew of no way to handle his grief other than to keep busy and continue on his path in Bozeman. Many well-wishers told him to just try to forget the misfortune—a common counsel of the time for deep personal loss.[223] [224] In time, baby boy Schubert June Dyche was taken to Salt Lake City to be cared for by his deceased mother's sister Venetia and her husband.[225]

There was another Bobcat birth that summer, as Frank and Mary Ward had their second child, Hal Green Ward. He was born on July 15, 1928, in plenty of time for Frank to concentrate on getting ready for his third season as a Bobcat basketball player. He was happy to have Schubert there as his new head coach.

21
1928–29 SEASON

Stand Up and Cheer

> *Stand up and cheer, / Cheer long and loud for dear Montana, /*
> *For today we raise, / The blue and gold to wave victorious, / Our sturdy band*
> *now is fighting, / And we are sure to win fray, / We've got the vim, /*
> *We're here to win, / For this is dear Montana's Day!*
> *—Montana State College fight song*[226]

In the fall of 1928, about 400 freshmen students came to Montana State College, an increase of around 100 from the year before. They were greeted by the return of Alfred Atkinson. The president had arrived back a few months before from his year sabbatical at Cornell University, where he completed the research work he had started there in 1912. He had also visited Europe. But his greatest satisfaction was getting back to his campus, where enrollment had swelled to just over 1,100 students, and Atkinson took pride in the possibility that his college might be as large as the University of Wyoming, the state's only four-year college. It was also important to the colleges in the area to field competitive athletic teams. Ott Romney was gone, and Atkinson did not yet have full confidence in Shubert Dyche. Atkinson's questions about Dyche's ability to handle the job still had to be answered. Wouldn't it be embarrassing if the Bobcats lost to BYU, showing the superiority of Romney and the weakness of the former East High School janitor whom Atkinson had just elevated to be his head coach?

In the meantime, as the golden glow of the Montana autumn was starting to appear, bright-eyed freshmen were arriving for fall quarter. Gathering on the lawns and reading the first edition of the campus paper, the *Exponent*, they learned that green beanie caps for men and green berets for women had to be worn by first-year students. In October, they would be required to paint the block "M" on the mountain face of the gap leading out of town to Bridger Canyon. The female students were also greeted with the good and bad news that the women's dormitory, which had vacancies the year before, was now full and turning young ladies away to board in town.[227]

Schubert Dyche, head coach. *1930* Montanan.

The Bobcat athletes knew that when they faced off against BYU in football and basketball, they would be facing the prospect of Schubert Dyche being outcoached by Ott Romney. Was their quiet, sometimes stammering, new head coach the real glue for the team and a man to whom the players would give their all? These questions would have to be answered as the year played out.[228] [229]

Meanwhile, out in Moscow, Idaho, Schubert was on the gridiron sidelines for his first game as Bobcat head coach. He still suffered from the upheaval he had endured, and he was awkward and quite unsure of himself, but he was faced with the task of taking full charge of the football team in its opening game. He paced up and down and looked the part of a head coach, but he was not yet comfortable in his new job.[230] When the ball changed hands and went over to the Bobcat offense, he made his first gameday decision and inserted three new players to run a new play he had designed. It worked, and suddenly, the anxiety lifted. His team prayed for him and then played for him, and in the end, they beat Idaho, 15–13. When the players gathered with their arms around Schubert, he knew the worst of his long nightmare was over. His shattered life could begin again.[231]

Dyche left his jitters behind him when he beat Idaho, but now the team came face-to-face with destiny. They had to face Ott Romney and BYU in a football game played on Saturday, November 3, in Bozeman. When the BYU Cougars took the field, a capacity crowd of 2,500 gave Romney a sportsmanlike hearty welcome, instead of the expected boos and catcalls. But they left no doubt of their support for the home Bobcats. Dyche's team won, 19–7, and he got the satisfaction of proving to the

The Bobcats run the football against the Idaho Vandals in the fall of 1928. This was Schubert Dyche's first head coaching duty. *1929* Montanan *yearbook*.

fans he could coach, His team had outgained the Cougars, 283 yards to 165.[232] After the game, Romney wrote Dyche, congratulating him on the trick play he had designed. It seems that Dyche had his team line up in punt formation on first down. While Romney's bewildered players were trying to figure out why the Bobcats were going to kick so early, they ran off a running play to score on their way to the victory.[233]

22

THE BOBCATS GRIEVE OVER A TEAMMATE'S DEATH AND ALMOST LOSE MAX WORTHINGTON TO RHEUMATIC FEVER

Montana State's outstanding intersectional game of the year was played against Nebraska's Cornhuskers at Lincoln, Nebraska.... This game was "Greenie" Worden's last appearance on the football field and it was the finest game of his career.
—*1928* Montanan

There had been a tragedy for the Bobcats during the football season. One of the players Schubert Dyche was relying on for a major contribution to the basketball team was Frank "Greenie" Worden, out of the Irish Catholic enclave in Butte, Montana. He had been a high school all-time, all-state player, along with Brick Breeden, and he was one of the best athletes from Montana schools in those days. He had been barely beaten out of a starting job on the basketball team by Max Worthington the season before when they were freshmen. Disaster struck when Worden started experiencing acute pain as the Bobcat football team was returning from a game at Nebraska. When the team reached Bozeman, he was rushed to the hospital with appendicitis. A doctor operated on him and then fought to keep him alive for three weeks. His teammates visited every day and crowded into the high-ceilinged, terrazzo-floored hospital hallway, only to have his mother come out of his room on a cold, dark November 10 to say that Frank had died.

To anyone from Bozeman who expected a Catholic funeral and Mass for someone from Butte with an Irish-sounding nickname, they soon found they were mistaken. His final rites were said at a small Mormon gathering. His parents were apparently among the small group of LDS Church members who had made their way to Montana from Utah.[234] After the funeral, his shaken teammates could only resolve to move on and dedicate their games to their fallen comrade. Coupled with the death of Schubert's wife, they now knew how serious life could be. They vowed to win every game the rest of the way for "Schube" and for "Greenie."[235]

Schubert Dyche had another worry, this one little known to the press and the public. While Max Worthington was lauded for his contributions as a freshman and heralded as a returner for the Bobcats, it was not generally known that he had actually been ruled inelibible for the coming Rocky Mountain Conference basketball season. One morning in late April, he had awoken with a severe sore throat. After gargling and sucking on an orange, he was sure it would go away, but it did not. During the day, he went to his classes and then to the gym to shoot baskets. The soreness persisted, and when he found he did not have energy enough to play basketball, his teammates finally persuaded him to seek medical attention at the hospital. A throat culture indicated streptococcus, and he was given penicillin. To him, it seemed like a repeat of a severe fever he had experience in Billings when he was eleven, but he was sure it would not develop into that. He took the pills he had been prescribed and rested for a few days, during which he thought there were periods of remission, indicating the infection was leaving. But it didn't work out that way, and on May 8, he was delirious and taken to the hospital with a high fever. He stayed there the next ten days, sometimes almost unconscious, until the fever broke. At almost the same time, he was losing his hair because of it. The diagnosis of rheumatic fever sent fear through him, his teammates and Dyche, for all of them knew it could cause permanent heart damage.

During his hospitalization, Max's parents came from Billings and spent long hours at his

Max Worthington. *1928 Montanan.*

bedside. His grandmother had come with them, and she rented a small apartment on Willson Avenue where she could live and take care of Max after he was out of the hospital. When he was discharged, he stayed with her for several weeks. Too weak to attend his classes, Max lost all his credits for the quarter, and the Rocky Mountain Conference declared him ineligible to play basketball during the 1928–29 season.

Max and Schubert appealed the conference decision and then waited anxiously for the delegates to take up the matter at their meeting on October 6. They did not have enough time to do it then, and again on October 8 they failed to make a decision. Finally, during the two-day December meeting in Salt Lake City at the magnificent Hotel Utah, next to the Deseret Gym, a majority of those in attendance voted to restore his eligibility; three of the twelve members voted against it. It was in the nick of time for the opening of the 1929 conference season, and both Schubert and Max breathed a sigh of relief.[236][237]

Schubert was elated by the decision, as he had already started basketball practices in the early fall and Max was an essential part of the plans to win another Rocky Mountain Conference championship. With Frank Worden now only a sad memory, Schubert Dyche set out to reconsider his starting five. He had been thinking about a move of the talented Worthington to starting forward to pair with Cat Thompson, but Max was too good as a guard to weaken that position. The answer Schubert came up with was to elevate the maturing Orland Ward to starting status at forward to pair with Cat. Frank Ward was back at center with his "usual bag full of tricks" to pull on the opposition when the season started. Brick Breeden would again pair with Worthington in the backcourt.

Dyche was still not overly confident that the 1929 team would do as well as the 1928 team had, even though they were basically the same players. Their lopsided wins over the Livingston Railway Club and the Hardin Moose didn't inspire confidence in anyone. "Teams have tried again and again to remain at the top of the ladder year after year but they have failed," he said. That was the bottom side. On the top side, Schubert objectively knew there was at least a chance at greatness. Many thought the Cats would certainly be a wonder team if they could take the championship again this year to make it three in a row.[238]

23

THE COOK PAINTERS COME TO TOWN

As a starter let it be announced that what the New York Yankees are in baseball, what Notre Dame is in football, what Bobby Jones is in golf, what Bill Tilden is in tennis, that is what the Cook Paint team is in basketball.[239]
—Montana Standard *(Butte, MT), January 4, 1929*

This was not the right time to have a Bobcat letdown, and Schubert was having none of it, because that year there was something very big in the offing. He had been contacted by the Cook Painters, an independent team from Kansas City, Missouri, proposing a three-game series that could be played in Montana. This was not to be taken lightly. The Painters, or the "Cook Paint Boys," as their uniforms read, were the national-champion AAU team sponsored by the Cook Paint Company. They were coming off a winning season after playing the best teams in the country. The players on the team had all starred in college and were continuing to be stars with the Painters. Their leading player was Forrest "Red" DeBernardi, who many considered the country's best basketball player. He and his teammates would certainly come to Montana expecting to win resoundingly, and Dyche knew that for the Bobcats this would be their ultimate test. It was up to him and his team to improve their play in the games they had scheduled before the juggernaut from Kansas City arrived.

The Bobcat fans in Bozeman were at first skeptical of a team from a paint company in Kansas City. After all, what was a paint company doing with a basketball team? Soon, the *Montana Standard* in Butte answered the question, and Bozeman knew that after the Bobcats returned from a road trip, they might be watching the World Series of basketball.[240]

With the Cook Painters still a few weeks away, the Bobcats started the season with three exhibition games, all of which they won handily; one against the Livingston Railway team (73–19) and two against the Hardin Moose (90–28 and 59–21).

The Bobcat team took to the rails during Christmas break and chugged south to play the Colorado State Teachers in Greeley. Cat Thompson and Frank Ward, with precision, broke through an immobile defense to score, and in the end the game was a runaway for the Cats, 59–29. Schubert made sure all the team members saw the floor in the first game. They could have played down to the Teachers' level in the second game, but they didn't, and even though their shots were not falling, the Teachers were worse, and they lost, 58–31.[241] Then it was back home in Bozeman, where the Bobcats overpowered an in-state opponent, Montana School of Mines. That team had taken the train to Bozeman, where they were beaten, 58–11.[242] After that, it was the Livingston Railway team again (96–15). Those who saw the game uncomfortably witnessed a physical mauling—the lone referee saw fit to call only one foul on the Bobcats.[243]

Taking but a brief time off after Christmas, the Bobcats boarded the train again, this time for Walla Walla, Washington, to play two games, one on New Year's Day and another on the following day, against Whitman College. During the games, Schubert could see Brick Breeden move under the Whitman basket time and again to block the path of a driving player, interrupt passes and collect a treasure trove of defensive rebounds. His outlet passing to Max Worthington on the sidelines was flawless. Even then, the Bobcats could not get their publicized fast break fully in gear, and they scored only 45 points in each game, a tribute to Whitman's defense. But Whitman's vaunted offense scored only 42 points in the first game and just 30 in the second, and the Bobcats left with two wins.

The next day, January 3, the Bobcats got off their train under a cold, gray, misty sky in Pullman on the South Fork of the Palouse River that wound through town. Above the river, on the top of a hill, was Washington State College, home of the onetime national champion Cougars, the team that back in 1917 Ott Romney thought he might be able to emulate someday. The Bobcats knew they would be in for a battle, and they were up to it. Orland and Frank Ward both had good scoring nights in leading the team, which had 43 points. Brick Breeden and the defense held the Cougars to only 31 points.

As the Bobcats looked around during the Washington State games, they could see spectators with letterman jackets bearing the chenille block letter "I." They soon found out that these were the Vandals from the University of Idaho, only about eight miles away across the state line in Moscow. They had made the short trip to get the measure of the Bobcats, whom they would be playing soon. In fact, they would be playing the Bobcats in the same gym they were in at Washington State. The Vandals' new Gothic-Revival gymnasium was not yet ready for play. What the Idaho Vandals team and fans saw in the Bobcat game against the Cougars could not have given them confidence, even though they knew that in the previous season they had given the Bobcats one of their only two losses in thirty-eight games.[244]

In their first game against the Vandals, it was all Cat Thompson for the Bobcats as he unveiled an uncanny array of shots in scoring 21 points to equal the entire Vandal team's output in a 44–21 victory. It embarrassed the proud Vandals, who had scored 46 and then 44 points against the Bobcats the previous season. In the second game, Thompson broke loose again with another 21 points. The Bobcat defense held, and with the help of second-half rally, they won, 54–40.[245]

The next morning, the Montana State team left the Palouse on the train for a day's travel back to Bozeman. They knew a weighty challenge would soon face them there. It would turn out to be perhaps the most important challenge they would have as a team.[246]

The Cook Painters were not frightened by the prospect of playing the Bobcats in Montana. As it turned out, the Cook Paint Company had everything to do with basketball that year, as it had the previous year. As the rank and file Bozeman sports fans soon learned, the Painters won it all and had captured the national Amateur Athletic Union championship the year before, beating competitors from all over the country. The AAU was the gold standard in the country; it had been conducting the National Men's Basketball Championship since 1897.[247]

As they dug deeper, the business boosters in Bozeman learned that the Cook Paint Company in Kansas City was one of the largest paint manufacturers in the United States. Its basketball team had one of the best-known players in the nation, Forrest "Red" DeBernardi, who had signed with them to be both a player and the team coach with the goal of winning the AAU championship.[248] The team (officially known as the Cook Paint Boys) won the national AAU title in 1928, making it the best team in the United States at a time when professional basketball took a back seat to the teams of former college players fielded by large industrial companies. The AAU teams competed not only against the best college teams in the country but also against their industrial counterparts. These teams gave their corporate sponsors tremendous advertising on a national scale, and the owners of the firms employed the players for their basketball abilities.

Bozeman fans got shocked into reality as the papers brought them this information, and word began to circulate around town that the Cooks were the best team in the United States at any level. The Bobcats could have used Coach Ott Romney's outgoing confidence, but he was gone. In his place, the reticent Schubert Dyche offered only the lukewarm conclusion that the Bobcats could win.

DeBernardi, the former college great, usually played at forward to take advantage of his scoring ability. However, when the Painters heard of Cat Thompson, it became known that DeBernardi would move to guard for the games against the Bobcats so that he could match up with Thompson as a defender and try to keep him under wraps.[249] This game was shaping up to be the battle of the gladiators, and the people in Bozeman could feel that something very important was coming. On January 10, when the Cook Painters came out on the floor in the gymnasium, the Bozeman fans gasped. Their center, Vic Holt, was six feet, seven inches tall, and some said he appeared to be about half a foot taller than Frank Ward. The difference became most apparent when they lined up for center jumps, which, surprisingly, Frank could win sometimes. Holt was not only big but also talented. He had been the national college player of the year the previous season at the University of Oklahoma. Cat Thompson of course knew of him, because they had both been All-Americans in 1928, when Holt was with the Sooners.[250] During the games, Holt was sometimes used sparingly due to illness. Even in warm-ups, the fans could see that he exhibited the moves and quick feet of a smaller man. He had a reputation as a fearless rebounder, getting in position under the basket and using his height and long arms to grab rebounds, sometimes tipping in his team's missed shots and controlling the boards on the defensive end. But Holt had a weakness that showed even in warm-ups. Schubert Dyche observed that he was not a very good shot from farther out. To a man, the Bobcats agreed that Holt should be kept away from the basket, and they started preparing for the physical abuse they would have to take in doing that.

With Holt in the post, the Cooks had their full offense available in the first game, and they executed their game plan perfectly, even helped by luck. At one point, DeBernardi lunged for a ball going out of bounds, controlled it and, as he was falling, heaved it blindly toward the basket. It went in! The

Painters had a 16-point lead at the half. Both Max Worthington and Orland Ward had been ill but, if needed, were prepared to come in for the second half. In the dressing room at halftime, a calm Schubert Dyche addressed his team and laid out his plan. Since Holt was on his game and playing close to the basket, he decided that Breeden and Ward would double-team him. The others would form a triangular zone defense down low. Breeden's long arms grabbed at the ball when Holt attempted to fake, and on many occasions he tied up the big man for a jump ball. If Holt drove off the post, Frank Ward remained in front of him, blocking his route to the basket. Shubert had also told the Bobcats that they had to shoot quickly if they were going to catch up and even the score. This worked. The Bobcats rushed the Painters off their feet and doubled the scoring output, 24 points to 12. All looked well until the Bobcats' shots failed to go in during the closing minute. The Bobcats were close, but they left the floor as losers by a score of 44–40.

In the second game, on Friday, January 11, the Bobcats didn't expect to lose again. They planned to have both Orland and Max back at full strength. But by game time, neither was well enough to take the floor, so the Bobcats played without them. On the opponent's side, Victor Holt was not well enough to play, so both teams took the floor at less than full strength.[251] The Bobcats played even with the Painters in the first half as each team started conservatively, cautiously holding on to the ball. In the second half, Coach Dyche cut the Bobcats loose, and the Cooks barely had time to catch their breath from the feverish pace. Relying on the quickness of Thompson, the Bobcats broke out to a big lead and couldn't be stopped. It was something the team needed, and it was somewhat expected that Brick Breeden played despite an illness. The 17-point loss was the Cooks' first of the season.[252] [253] The series was now tied one game apiece.[254]

Losing to a college team did not sit well with DeBernardi, who had the added weight of being the coach of his team. He spent the rest of the late evening pondering their performance, but all he could come up with was that he should not have kept Victor Holt out of the game and that Cat Thompson and Frank Ward were great players, even better than those the Painters played against regularly in their tough AAU league. But DeBernardi, at age thirty, was self-effacing, and he blamed himself for the loss and questioned his own coaching judgment.

The teams moved on to Butte for a Sunday-afternoon game on January 13 in the gym at the Montana School of Mines, which floated airily on a steep, wind-swept hill above the town, encased in the crystalline air of a below-zero day. The Cooks got off to an early 10–3 lead despite the Bobcats'

1929 Basketball National Champions

close and swarming defense. The crafty DeBernardi was doing a good job defending Thompson until Frank Ward pivoted around Holt as though he was going for the basket, instead passing to the streaking Cat, who swept in for his first basket. The Cooks responded with two tip-in baskets by Holt, who had gotten the ball down low twice and tipped his own missed shots back in over the top of Frank Ward, who was elbowed and claimed he was fouled, but the referee didn't call it.

The determined Bobcats called a time-out on the floor and huddled around Schubert Dyche on the sidelines. The coach had been quietly observant during the first two games, and he now thought he detected a weakness in the Painter defense. Instead of Frank Ward pivoting left on Holt when he had the ball in the high post, he thought he could take advantage of Holt's reaction to the play in previous games. Dyche told Frank to take a step left and pass the ball back to Max Worthington almost as soon as he got it. By this time, Holt would have already transferred his weight to his left foot, and Max could dribble by him with Holt still off-balance, being left only to grab at him. At this point, Frank could roll to his left around Holt and take a pass from Max, and with Cat Thompson cutting hard for the basket, Frank could hit him with a pass good for a layup. This worked twice; the third time, Thompson was fouled and made the free throw. Then it was Frank's turn to drive all the way to the basket, followed by a play in which he fed Orland the ball for a layup. All of a sudden, the Golden Bobcats were ahead, 18–15.

Max Worthington had the natural qualities of speed, strength, quickness and shooting ability to fit in well as the floor guard on the Golden Bobcats. He was the youngest starting player on the team and was a four-year all-conference player in the Rocky Mountain Conference. *Courtesy Montana State University Special Collections Photo Archives.*

An energized Holt, embarrassed at being beaten, powered for an offensive rebound and tipped the ball in for a basket. A moment later, with the pace still frenetic, Frank Ward was fouled and scored, but then a lanky Cook guard swept through the Bobcat defense twice for pretty baskets just as the half ended. But the Cats were still ahead, 21–19. They went to the locker room with their fate as the "wonder team" of the West still in the balance.

At halftime, the Bobcats reflected on the fact that the Cooks were an experienced team full of canny veterans with years of experience, and they were not likely to take defeat by an upstart college team sitting down. It was not only their pride that was on the line, but also possibly their jobs at Cook Paint, where they were hired to play basketball and required to do little else but win. Management would not like to see its exquisite basketball team lose after investing in their success. Schube and the Bobcats had to do something, and they had to devise a strategy. In the first half, Holt had been extremely rough and aggressive, which cost him two fouls of the four allotted. As the Bobcats huddled, ready for the second half, Schubert emphasized that they needed to look for an opportunity to get Holt to foul out. At that point, Max Worthington spoke up with an idea of how he could make that happen. Coming out for the second half, Max dribbled right at Holt with a lowered shoulder, knocking the big man off his balance, which he regained enough to punch at Max with both hands. The blows bounced off, but it appeared to be the start of a major altercation as Frank Ward, the former boxer, rushed over to Max's defense. The referee soon calmed the combatants down, assessing fouls on both Max and Victor Holt. It was Max's first, but it was Holt's third. The strategy worked, and since four fouls disqualified a player in those days, Holt would have to be careful to stay in the game. He was now the only Painter who seemed to be able to score. But it was better to foul him than let him score. Sometimes double-teaming worked in getting steals, but it also brought fouls on the Bobcats. In the end, it was Breeden's long arms on defense that stymied the Cooks. With Frank and Max surrounding Holt in the high post, Brick Breeden patrolled under the basket, bodily moving the Cook players who tried to penetrate, blocking shots, changing trajectories, stealing the ball and sweeping in for rebounds to hold down the scoring of everyone but Holt.

As the game came down to the wire, the Painters were trailing by five points. They were desperate for a last stand, and Holt answered the call, making a spectacular falling-away jump shot from uncharacteristic medium range that was followed by back-to-back baskets by the Painters, giving them a 6-point run to take the lead.

Schubert Dyche called a time-out. He had seen something else now in the Painter team. They had become comfortable in their established zone defense, and Schubert instructed his team to disrupt the zone by using more cuts and passes. That resulted in the Ward brothers doing some fancy passing and equally creative shooting, giving the Bobcats a comfortable 10-point lead that saw them through the remainder of the game. They had been moving so fast that Holt and the others could only grab at them, and finally, Holt and one other Painter player fouled out. Schube's strategy to get rid of the powerful Victor Holt had worked. Cat Thompson had also left the game on over-the-back fouls because he had gone high to compete with Holt for rebounds despite being the smallest player on the floor. The Bobcats defeated the Painters again soundly, 46–34, and won the series.[255]

Word of the victory sped across the nation, with newspapers reporting on the prowess of the Bobcats and particularly Cat Thompson.[256][257] The Rocky Mountain Conference season was now upon the Bobcats. As a team, they were well prepared, having played stiff competition in the preseason and then beating the consensus nation's best, the Cook Painters.

24

THE BEST OF
THE CHAMPIONSHIP SEASON

"A Collection of Artists"

The past season has been the greatest and most successful season through which the Bobcats have ever played. Their spectacular basketball, combined with their 60-point-a-game average has brought national recognition to Montana State College. The team is simply a collection of artists, unsurpassable in their field.
—*1929* Montanan

Cat Thompson was not one to brood, but behind his inscrutable countenance he had a vendetta. At Dixie College in St. George, Utah, he had played with Lorraine Cox, a good player who could hold his own with anyone. And Lorraine had impressed Utah's coach, Vidal Peterson, who glowingly talked about having him on the Ute team. In fact, Cox got more coverage from the Utah newspapers as a leading player in the Rocky Mountain Conference than Cat did from his outpost location in Montana. One day in January, Cat opened an envelope addressed to him in Bozeman from someone in La Verkin. They had sent a newspaper clipping that caused him to bristle. There in the *Iron County Record* of Parowan he read: "The Cat is no better known than Lorraine Cox, University of Utah Redskin. By the time the sweet little Ute player gets pouring the goals through the hoop, Rocky Mountain conference fans will be calling him Rain."[258] But the sportswriter did not know Cat's determination that set him to making sure that before the season was over no one would ever compare Lorraine Cox to him in any way. Actually, Cat knew and liked Cox, who had always looked up to him, and Cox remembered the 1925 team at Dixie that

1929 Basketball National Champions

included Ashworth (before he became known as Cat). According to Cox: "Those guys were a real inspiration to us. They were fast and they were sure shots and we wanted to be just like them."[259]

Fresh off their heady Sunday victory to end the Cook series, the Bobcats headed for a midweek game in Missoula against the archrival Montana Grizzlies. Schubert had cautioned his team against a letdown, but it did not happen. Cat Thompson was still on his game and scored 23 points. He had nine field goals by going over, through and around the slower defenders. Brick Breeden and Max Worthington, from their usually low-scoring guard positions, had 7 and 6 points, respectively, and Frank Ward had only 9 points, but it gave the Bobcats a 46–34 victory.[260]

The Utah State Aggies were prepared when the Bobcats showed up in Logan on a wintery day on Friday, January 18. Getting off to an early lead, the fine-tuned Bobcats coasted to a 57–38 win. A well-rested Orland Ward, who had been held out of the Missoula game because of injury, led the team with 21 points, and Cat Thompson, his running mate at forward, had 13, with sixteen field goals between them. Frank Ward had a solid 9 points and was fouled frequently when he was shooting, resulting in five free throws. Schubert Dyche was happy for the win, but he knew he was up against Dick Romney, Ott's brother, whom he admired as a coach. And he knew that Dick's team, loaded with talent, could come back at any time—and they did. Stung by Orland's output in the first game, the Aggies clamped down on him and his scoring. He was limited to a single free throw. Cat, too, was well guarded, but his uncanny shooting produced 18 points. Frank had 13, but the result was disappointing, as the Bobcats lost, 47–43.[261]

Brick Breeden. *Courtesy Montana State University Special Collections Photo Archives.*

No loses were being tolerated on the Bobcat team, and after the game, Schubert calmly talked to his team about their performance and where he thought they could do better. Confident in him now as their coach, the Bobcats to a man pledged that they would not lose another game that season and would come out ready to play every game and not overlook any

Montana State's Golden Bobcats

Left: Cat Thompson, in a day when national statistics may not have been accurately kept, was, in addition to being the outstanding player in the country in 1929, was also considered the leading scorer. *Courtesy Montana State University Special Collections Photo Archives.*

Right: Brick Breeden, with his thirty-seven-inch arm length, was used as an intimidating defender who could singlehandedly shut down the scoring of the other team. He didn't score that much, nor was he required to do so, on a team with other players who were great scorers. His defense was known nationwide, and he was an All-American and a four-time all-conference player. *Courtesy Montana State University Special Collections Photo Archives.*

opponent. It was a tall order for a team that had just started their conference schedule. For Cat Thompson and the Ward brothers—the Utah trio from the "sticks" in southern Utah—it was a matter of their heritage to not lose to any of the three conference teams in Utah. For Brick Breeden and Max Worthington—the two starters from Montana—it was a matter of their competitive natures that they simply could not loose.

The next weekend, Ott Romney and the BYU Cougars entered the gym in Bozeman that years later would be named for him. He received an ambivalent reception when he led his team onto the floor. For every basketball fan who thought he had been the architect of the Golden Bobcats, there was an equal number who thought that Schubert Dyche had been the true genius all along. None of this controversy bothered the confident Ott or the introverted Schubert. The former had plenty of friends in Bozeman

1929 Basketball National Champions

who were not likely to change their minds, and the latter recognized only results, eschewing anything laudatory. As the fans watched the seemingly cordial greeting between the two coaches, it wasn't too apparent that the relationship between the two had been broken. Schubert hadn't gone to Utah with Ott, and Ott hadn't wholeheartedly endorsed Schubert as his replacement at MSC. As good a coach and mentor as Ott Romney had been, it was now becoming known around Bozeman that he was not the man directly responsible for getting Cat Thompson and the Ward brothers to Montana State. Schubert was. To make matters worse for Ott, he was considered someone who had left his Utah stars high and dry, even trying to take Schubert away from the team. In this fight, the fans' hearts would be with Schubert, whose personal life had been in disarray when he took over and who now had made a heroic comeback.

Coming out on the court, the Bobcats were grim-faced and determined, and to the embarrassment of Ott Romney, they doubled the score on his Cougars, 72–36. The team did not even need to rely much on Cat Thompson, as Orland Ward was stepping up and playing at a new level, matching Cat with 16 points and seven field goals. The Bobcats surprised Ott, who thought he knew the tendencies of his former players. He was outcoached by Schubert, who used his guards as scorers, rotating them with the forwards on some plays. Max Worthington ended with 11 points, and Brick Breeden had 13.[262]

The next night, Romney's Cougars did little better, losing again, 67–37, before the Bozeman home crowd, which had come to realize that the loss of Ott was not that bad. Frank Ward dominated the BYU center and scored eleven field goals, mostly by going over him on drives to the basket from the post. He had 24 points for the evening. Cat was his usual quick self, giving the BYU players fits, and he ended with 19 points. After the game, Ott, with a bit of an edge, congratulated Schubert on his victory, but there would always be

Orland Ward from Parowan, Utah, developed into an essential player on the 1929 Golden Bobcats. *Courtesy of Montana State University Special Collections Photo Archives.*

an unspoken tension between them. In no small measure, this was due to the clumsy handling by Romney of his departure from MSC the year before, when he thought, without asking, that Schubert would want to follow him to BYU. Happening as it did in the middle of Schubert's crisis with June Dyche's death in childbirth and with Ott really giving no help to Schubert in his quest to become head coach, the civility the two men had toward each other was superficial—and always would be.

Having beaten his old mentor, Schubert left Bozeman with his team the next morning on the train to Missoula. Along the way, he could see the familiar countryside flash by, and he thought that there were once again some good things in life. Maybe he would pick up his flute when he got home and practice a little to be ready the next time he had a chance to play with the MSC orchestra. These thoughts were soon interrupted by the necessity to take care of winning the mythical state title.

The Bobcats won the title without trouble, beating the archrival Montana Grizzlies, 62–18, in a game in which an injured Max Worthington did not play. In the next game, against Mount St. Charles (Carroll College) of Helena, Schubert almost made a mistake by holding Cat Thompson, Frank Ward and Brick Breeden out of a guaranteed victory that was almost lost before the Bobcats pulled it out, 37–34. Even with that scare, Schubert kept to his plan to use his reserves, and in a game against Montana Mines, he barely escaped with a 31–29 win.[263]

After the close calls, the strategy paid off, as the Bobcat starters proved to be rested and healed up from injuries enough to dominate the rest of the conference season. They would not overlook any team, as they had the Utah State Aggies in their earlier second game in Logan, and they would get a chance for revenge.

In their game on February 8 in Bozeman, they played with heightened intensity against Utah State again, and the Aggies were not up to the onslaught. Montana State took an early lead and never relinquished it, winning 53–29. The next night, it was even worse for Dick Romney's team, which lost by 44 points. The scoring of Cat, Frank and Orland did them in. The expatriate country kids from Utah scored 52 points between them. As good as the offense was for the Bobcats, the defense was almost better, and the final score was 69–25. It was an embarrassingly low total for Dick Romney and the Aggies, and he had to concede that the reason he caught the Bobcats for a loss earlier in Logan was because it was one of the worst nights for the visitors on the road. At least his brother Ott hadn't beaten him this time, because he was no longer there.[264]

1929 Basketball National Champions

It was now time for the Bobcats to play again against Utah, and on February 15, they met the Utes in Salt Lake City in Deseret Gym. It was a slow game, but the Bobcats won handily, 40–28, with Cat, Frank and Orland all scoring in the low double figures. The pace was picked up a little the next night, with Thompson scoring 16 and Frank Ward 13 as the Bobcats won, 51–43.

Then it was on to Provo, where Ott Romney welcomed his former team to BYU. In the game played on February 18, he had expected his Cougars to put up a good defense and be competitive. He might have done better trying to turn back the ocean tide. The game opened with Frank Ward controlling the center jump, as he usually did, and tipping the ball back to Max Worthington, who passed it to Brick Breeden. From half-court, Brick hit a streaking Cat Thompson with a bullet pass, and Cat scored on an uncontested layup. And so it went for the entire night, ending in a 70–42 Bobcat victory. By the end of the game, Cat, Orland and Frank between them had scored twenty-seven field goals, and Max and Brick had defended well. The loud crowd now seemed to know that Schubert Dyche was something more than a janitor.

The next night, February 19, Ott Romney was desperate. He double-teamed Thompson. It worked, and the magnificent Cat was held to 15 points for the game. The unintended consequence for Ott was that it freed up both of the Ward brothers to score their respective 23 and 22 points. Orland might have scored even more, but he fouled out. Ott had not been without at least a small effective strategy, as he found a way to get the ball inside down low and score even on the outstanding defense of Brick Breeden and Max Worthington. It gave his team 15 more points than the night before, and they lost by only 9 points, 66–57. Only Ott would consider that a moral victory.[265]

In Salt Lake City, the Utah supporters were now hopeful the Utes could keep the Bobcats from their third consecutive Rocky Mountain Conference title, but it would be a formidable task, since the last series was to be played in Bozeman.[266] Once there, the Utes stepped down from their train in Bozeman and got into cars to take them to their hotel. It was March 1, and they could hardly wait to get into the warmth of the Bobcats' gym, still a new building and adequately heated by steam transported in buried pipes from a central heating plant a block away. It was an inviting place for players and fans alike and helped get the Bozeman fans through the long winters.

The Utes had lost two games to the Bobcats in Utah just two weeks before, and their experience showed them that the fast-breaking Bobcat juggernaut could shoot their lights out if they had the ball. Vidal Peterson, their coach, knew it. In his private thoughts, he could bemoan the failure of his school to recruit Cat Thompson and the Ward brothers when they might have had a chance. This night, the Utes couldn't keep the ball away from the Bobcats or defend against their shooting, and Frank Ward scored eleven field goals and 22 points. The Utah coach would see his own well-defended team defeated, 63–47. The next night, March 2, the game seemed much the same. Cat Thompson scored 23 points and matched Frank Ward's eleven field goals from the night before.[267] The score was 63–47. With that, the Bobcats won their third straight Rocky Mountain Conference Western Division title.[268] They now had to play Colorado, from the Eastern Division, for the championship.

Before the title series, there was still time for the Bobcats to play more home games. The students, fans and the coach all wanted to see more of the amazing team—more of the choreographed set plays; more of the unchoreographed, rapidly flowing fast breaks; more of the force of Brick Breeden and Frank Ward as they dominated the backboards on opposite ends of the court; more of Max Worthington and Orland Ward as they grew each game into experienced players; and, above all, more of Cat Thompson, whose skill, agility, shooting, ball hawking and constant, full-throttle playing were becoming the talk of the nation and marking him by some as the best player in the country. Crowded together were three quickly scheduled exhibition games on consecutive days, all of which the Bobcats won, beating the Behrendt's All-Stars (91–29), the Havre All-Stars (110–10) and the Great Falls All-Stars (97–23). In all of these games, the Bobcats used their regulars. Schubert saw the matches as an opportunity to improve scoring averages, and it worked. Against Havre, Cat had seventeen field goals and 35 points. Against Great Falls, Frank had eleven field goals and 26 points. With that, the home season for the Bobcats was over. Arrangements and train reservations were made by the fans to follow the team to Colorado, the second time that season, for the playoff between the Western and Eastern Division winners.[269]

The city of Denver was treated to a fine preview of the MSC team when they arrived in Colorado to play Colorado University of Boulder. Their statistics showed that the Bobcats had amassed 2,056 points in thirty-four games, and they were nearing the end of a three-year run in which they had lost only six games in the over one hundred that they had played. Against the Bobcats, the stodgy, defense-minded Colorado team's only hope was to slow the game down and keep Cat Thompson and Frank Ward from scoring. To their peril, they did not recognize that they also had to contain Orland Ward, and they were blindsided.[270]

1929 Basketball National Champions

The Bobcats practice defense. *Courtesy Montana State University Special Collections Photo Archives.*

As the championship series against Colorado approached, basketball fans in Denver and Boulder were treated to detailed press coverage of the players on the Bobcat team, and the Colorado fans were exposed to Montana State's less-heralded forward, Orland Ward, who had blossomed into a scorer, particularly when Cat Thompson received extra attention on defense. In the first CU game, Orland broke loose for 21 points, and even though heavily guarded, Cat scored 19 points.[271] In the next game, on March 25, 1929, in Denver, the Colorado Buffaloes again failed to contain Cat Thompson and Orland Ward, and the Bobcats won the Rocky Mountain Conference championship by a lopsided score of 62–33.[272] A third game was on the schedule, so the teams played it anyway, with the score 53–47 in favor of the Golden Bobcats.[273]

25

THE NATIONAL CHAMPIONSHIP POSTSEASON

They have earned the state title, the Rocky Mountain Conference title, and having displayed their superiority over the famous Cook Painters there is no telling to what heights they might have climbed had it been possible for them to meet some of the so-called strong Eastern teams. Every man on the squad was a star. Tommy was chosen as All-American forward by Knute Rockne; Tommy, Frank Ward and Breeden were given places on the All-Conference team by the Associated Press, while…the sports editor for the Denver Post, placed Orland Ward with the other three on the All-Conference selection. In addition to this the three high scorers of the Rocky Mountains were Frank Ward, "Cat" Thompson and Orland Ward, in the order named.[274]
—*1929* Montanan

There was one more thing to consider before calling the season over. Shubert Dyche had received an unusual invitation. The Cook Painters, smarting from their loss of the series in Montana, challenged the Bobcats to another three-game series. Mr. Cook did not like the negative publicity his team earned from losing to the Bobcats, and he was ready to risk another meeting, even though it might mean more losses. But he didn't think so. In his mind, his team was superior, and he wanted to prove it.

On Wednesday, March 20, the papers carried the decision of Coach Dyche not to play the Cooks again. It wasn't avoidance. At that time, the Cats were preparing for the three-game series for the Rocky Mountain Conference championship in Denver, which would put the Bobcats up to thirty-eight

1929 Basketball National Champions

Frank Ward was the center of the Golden Bobcats. His height was listed at six feet, two inches, which was considered tall for the time. He was a two-time All-American and a four-time all-conference player. *Courtesy Montana State University Special Collections Photo Archives.*

games for the season, and that was enough for any team. A second factor was that the Cook series would have extended the season into April, and unlike the Cook players, who were employees of the company, the college students on the Bobcat team had to finish their schoolwork.[275] The decision not to play the Cooks was final, and with that, the 1928–29 season was at an end.

And then came worrisome news. Someone had picked up the *Salt Lake City Tribune* and read a column written by Al Warden. The venerable sportswriter had never been a Bobcat friend. Bozeman readers went into shock as they heard that their Golden Bobcat team, the wonder team of the West and the pride of Bozeman and Montana, might be gone before the next season started. According to the *Tribune*, two industrial firms in Kansas City had seen an opportunity to compete right away in their AAU league against the likes of the Cook Painters.[276] Someone had figured out that all they had to do was steal away the Golden Bobcats, give the players jobs and put them on the court. The players named were Cat Thompson, the Ward brothers and Brick Breeden. Only Max Worthington, who was still a youngster, was not included in the rumor. The source of the story, according to Warden, came from Bozeman. Indeed, a hint of a rumor had been going around the Elks Club and the downtown Bozeman bars, where some of the boosters hung out. The rumor had the stuff of being more than mere speculation, but it was never confirmed that the players were actively considering it. In the end, when school was over for the year and Brick Breeden graduated, the remaining players agreed among themselves that they would be back next year to achieve even greater things.[277] They did not know then that there was nothing greater they could do than what they had achieved that season, nor would they achieve even that equal ever again.

26

DECISION TIME FOR CAT THOMPSON

He has yet to meet the guard who can effectively hold him down.
—1929 Montanan

There was some concern at the end of the year about whether Cat Thompson would be back for his fourth season. The reason was that he had already graduated. When he came to Montana State in the fall of 1926, he had brought with him his transcript from Dixie College, his junior college in St. George, Utah. He presented it to the registrar, who combed through his credits, aware of Cat's basketball reputation. The transcript revealed that Cat had been busy academically and had some attendance at the junior college for two years, not just one. In the end, the MSC registrar gave him fifty-eight advanced standing credits for his previous work. Now, in the spring of 1929, after only three full years of college work at MSC, Cat had enough credits to graduate, so he applied for a degree and was accepted. He proudly walked with the class of 1929 to receive his diploma. The question of what he should do the next year was before him. His coach, Schubert Dyche, had always favored education for education's sake. Cat's options were to play for an AAU team (several teams had contacted him) or continue playing for the Bobcats despite having graduated. Schubert assured him that he could register as a regular student, and that is what Cat did. But this time, he picked an even harder schedule than he had undertaken in his third year. In the fall, he signed up for upper-class courses in zoology, botany and bacteriology and continued in the same vein for the remainder of the year. He was not seeking a degree in that field, but he was challenging himself academically. Despite playing another grueling thirty-five-game schedule, he finished with all As and Bs. He was listed again in the 1930 yearbook as a graduating senior in health and physical education, the same thing he had graduated with the year before. But his transcript showed that he had only the single degree from MSC granted in 1929.[278]

EPILOGUE

After winning the consensus 1929 national championship and having three years of playing time together, the now-famous Golden Bobcats were ready to repeat in 1930, which would have made for an even more triumphal end to their story. But not all stories end in grand fashion, and their 1930 season disappointed some. They had taken a Christmas barnstorming trip to the Midwest and played well but lost to Butler—Cat Thompson and Frank Ward fouled out at the start of the second half—and Loyola. They won at Purdue, Marquette and Penn State.

Against the 1928 national champion Pittsburgh team, they were tied until the end, when the home team scored a needed basket. Criticism of refereeing came even from a Pittsburgh fan, but there were other factors. The trip to Pittsburgh had been long and hard, and the Bobcats were tired.

More important, the Bobcats lost Brick Breeden to graduation. Both Cat Thompson and Frank Ward were named All-Americans in 1930, but without the defensive presence of Breeden for the year, they lost 10 games against 26 wins, still a good record, but not as good as the identical 38-2 records of the previous two years. Pittsburgh's record was better, and they won the head-to-head competition so they were named the national champion for 1930.

Not all stories end perfectly, and this one had its downside. Schubert Dyche coached the 1929 champions and almost won the title again in 1930, but that was the height of his coaching career at Montana State. There was always a question whether the 1929 team should be credited to him as the recently elevated assistant coach, or whether it should be credited to Ott Romney.

Epilogue

Frank and Mary Ward and their two sons, Hal (*second from right*) and Jim. *Courtesy Montana State University Special Collections Photo Archives.*

Schubert's personality may have spelled trouble for him, because in 1938, while he was still serving as director of athletics and head coach, students at Montana State petitioned for his removal, citing personality problems and mismanagement of the department. The students did not succeed, but Schubert quit coaching basketball. As for his personal life, his wife, Ruth, had died in 1928, and he remarried in 1931 to Lillian Lutes of Butte. They remained married until she filed for divorce in 1952, citing extreme cruelty, one of the statutory grounds for divorce in Montana at the time.[279]

After they left the MSC campus, all of the starters of the 1929 team remained in Montana, except Orland Ward, who returned to Utah to coach at Parowan High for a time. He then took an administrative position at the University of Wyoming. Frank Ward coached at different schools and ended up in Red Lodge, Montana, where he was known to have had a trout-fishing farm and managed the Elks Club. In addition, he was for a while in an administrative job at Montana State and coached at Holy Rosary Catholic High School in Bozeman for a short time, during which he coached against the author's high school team from White Sulphur Springs, Montana. Sadly, word circulated among those familiar with the family that Mary Ward was not doing well and had to spend time in a rehabilitation facility. She passed away in 1950 and is buried in the Red Lodge cemetery with a headstone that identifies her only as "Mother Mary." It is dedicated by her sons "Hal" and "Jim," with no mention of a family name and no mention of Frank Ward.

NOTES

Introduction

1. *Salt Lake Tribune*, January 27, 1929.
2. *Daily Herald*, Sunday, January 27, 1929.

Chapter 1

3. Grant, *Teachings of the Presidents*.
4. Sanderson, "Cat Thompson."
5. Reeve, "Little Oasis in the Desert."
6. Alder and Brooks, *History of Washington County*; Bradshaw, *Under Dixie Sun*.
7. Sanderson, "Cat Thompson"; Webb, *Brief History of the La Verkin*.
8. Sanderson, "Cat Thompson."
9. See Sanderson, "Cat Thompson," on his basketball ability; see Grant, *Teachings of the Presidents*, on the message from Heber Grant.
10. Bradshaw, *Under Dixie Sun*.
11. Sanderson, "Cat Thompson."
12. Cat Thompson was still learning his unusual basketball techniques.
13. Ibid.; see John Ashworth Thompson transcript for schoolwork at Dixie.
14. Sanderson, "Cat Thompson."
15. Ibid.
16. Ibid.

17. Author conversations with Wendy Lisonbee, whose father, Gale Stulk of Parowan, was Frank Ward's nephew.
18. Sanderson, "Cat Thompson."

Chapter 2

19. Romney, *Off the Job Living*.
20. Poll, *Utah's History*.
21. Sheltra, *100 Things*; *Salt Lake Tribune*, May 4, 1973.
22. Romney, *"Dick."*
23. *Salt Lake Tribune* (obituary), May 4, 1973.
24. Sheltra, *100 Things*.
25. "Fred Bennion," Wikipedia.
26. Romney, *"Dick."*
27. Romney, *Off the Job Living*.

Chapter 3

28. *Salt Lake City Telegram*, October 6, 1914.
29. Rydell, et al., *In the People's Interest*, particularly 16, 17.
30. Ibid.
31. Wikipedia, "Fred Bennion."
32. *Salt Lake City Tribune*, March 21, 1914.
33. *Montanan* 1916 yearbook.
34. *Ogden Standard*, February 16, 1916.
35. Ibid; *Salt Lake Telegram*, October 19, 1914.
36. *Ogden Standard*, February 16, 1916; *Salt Lake Telegram*, October 19, 1914.
37. *Montanan* 1917 yearbook; George Ottinger Romney transcript.
38. MacAlduff, "A History."

Chapter 4

39. "Great Depression Transforms Montana"; Cooper, *From Tent Town to City*.
40. U.S. World War I Draft Registration Cards, 1917–1918 for G. Ottinger Romney, Montana, Yellowstone County, Draft Cards, Ancestry.com.
41. *Ronan Pioneer*, October 26, 1917, page 2.

42. "East Siders Hand Billings Real Trimming," *Salt Lake Telegram*, December 1, 1916.
43. *Salt Lake Telegram*, January 30, 1917; January 31, 1917.

Chapter 5

44. Malone, et al., *Montana*. The author's father, Paul R. Wylie Sr. of Bozeman, then nineteen years old, was on the East Coast in 1918 waiting with the army to be sent overseas to battle when the flu hit him and his battalion. He lay helplessly in an army infirmary, watching the young men in beds on either side die before his fever broke and he was spared.
45. "Four Athletic Brothers of the Romney Family in the Service," *Salt Lake Telegram*, August 13, 1918.
46. *Billings Gazette*, April 14, 1918.
47. *Salt Lake Telegram*, April 8, 1918, and April 10, 1919.
48. Montana County Marriages 1865–1950, Ancestry.com.
49. *Salt Lake Telegram*, April 8, 1918.
50. U.S. World War I Draft Registration Cards, 1917–1918 for Schubert Reilly Dyche, dated June 5, 1917, Ancestry.com.
51. From the author's conversation with Schubert Dyche's nephew, Stephen Dyche, PhD, a professor at Appalachian State University.
52. Romney, *Off the Job Living*.

Chapter 6

53. Rydell, et al., *In the People's Interest*.
54. From author's conversations with Bozeman architect George Mattson; see Smith, *Bozeman and the Gallatin Valley*; Rydell, et al., *In the People's Interest*.
55. Ibid.
56. Initiative 19.
57. United States Department of the Interior, National Register of Historic Places Registration Form, NPS Form 10-900.
58. Initiative 19.
59. Massachusetts Institute of Technology in Cambridge, Massachusetts.
60. United States Department of the Interior, National Register of Historic Places, Montana State University Historic District, 1965, Section 8, page 48.
61. Ibid.; 1917 Carsley/Gilbert Campus Plan.

Chapter 7

62. "Dyche Once Toured with Orchestra," *Greeley (CO) Daily Tribune*, September 4, 1942.
63. Ancetry.com.
64. *Carbondalian*, Saturday, March 26, 1892.
65. *Topeka Daily Capital*, March 24, 1892.
66. Ancestry.com.
67. *Topeka Daily Capital*, November 9, 1906.
68. "A Grocer Quits Business—E.A. Dyche of West Sixth Street Missing—No Reason Is Known," *Kansas Farmer and Mail and Breeze*, November 17, 1906.
69. U.S. Census, 1900 and 1910. Ancestry.com.
70. "Pueblo Has Been Developed into Great Steel City by Vast Industry of the Colorado Fuel and Iron Co.," *Christian Science Monitor*, September 17, 1909.
71. Edward Dyche family, Ancestry.com.
72. Schubert Reilly Dyche transcript.
73. 1910 U. S. Census.
74. Schubert Reilly Dyche transcript.
75. 1910 U.S. Census, Ancestry.com.
76. U.S. Army Transport Service, Passenger Lists, 1931–1939, Ancestry.com.
77. Utah U.S. Military Records, 1861–1970, Ancestry.com.
78. Roberts, *Jack Dempsey*.
79. *Coloradoan* University of Colorado Yearbook, 1919.
80. U.S. World War I Draft Registration Cards, 1917–1918 for Schubert Reilly Dyche, dated June 5, 1917, Ancestry.com.
81. *Salt Lake Tribune*, January 28, 1939.
82. *Salt Lake Telegram*, May 15, 1921.
83. The author played several games there himself in 1960 as part of a company basketball league. Having recently graduated from Montana State College, it was his impression that Deseret Gym was not as well appointed as the Bobcat gym.
84. Schubert Reilly Dyche transcript.
85. "Mexican Baseball Source of Pride South of the Border," National Baseball Hall of Fame, https://baseballhall.org.
86. University of Utah Archives, "Rocky Mountain Faculty Athletic Conference Records, Acc. 79."

Chapter 8

87. Allen, *My Basketball Bible*.
88. "Wilson Sporting Goods," Wikipedia.
89. Ibid.
90. "Wilson Sporting Goods Company History," Funding Universe.
91. Hill and Baron, *Amazing Basketball Book*.
92. *Billings Gazette*, December 29, 1926.
93. "Basketball," Encyclopedia.com.

Chapter 9

94. *Montanan* 1923 yearbook.
95. *Salt Lake City Tribune*, July 2, 1922.
96. *Montanan* 1923, 1924 yearbooks.
97. "List of Helms Foundation National Champions," Coaches Database, https://www.coachesdatabase.com.
98. Ibid. See also "Premo-Porretta National Champions," Coaches Database, https://www.coachesdatabase.com.

Chapter 10

99. *Salt Lake Telegram*, December 3, 1922.
100. *Anaconda (MT) Standard*, August 20, 1922; June 2, 1924.
101. *The Butte Miner* (Butte, Montana), February 7, 1924.

Chapter 11

102. Jacob Breeden was born on August 15, 1869, in Roscoe, St. Clair County, Missouri, and died on July 13, 1954, in Bozeman, Gallatin County, Montana, Ancestry.com.
103. U.S. Census, 1920. See *Glasgow (MT) Courier*, August 9, 1918, for more family details.
104. 1920 Polk Bozeman City Directory, house address: 414 South Tenth Street.

105. "Gus" Wylie was Robert Harold Wylie, the author's uncle. See *Great Falls Tribune*, October 23, 1921.
106. *Great Falls Tribune*, March 11, 1925.
107. *Montanan* 1929 yearbook.

Chapter 12

108. *Montanan* 1926 yearbook, "Basketball 1926."
109. Ibid.
110. "About Pacific," University of the Pacific; "University of the Pacific," Wikipedia.
111. *Montanan* 1926 yearbook.
112. Ibid.
113. Ibid.
114. Romney and Dyche had been successful just a couple of years previous in persuading Val Glynn, a big man who had played for them at East High School in Salt Lake City, to come north and play for the Bobcats.
115. *Billings Gazette*, December 29, 1926.

Chapter 13

116. Parowan High School Yearbook, "High School Song."
117. Seegmiller, *History of Iron County*.
118. Gerlach, *Alma Richards*.
119. Ibid; *Deseret News*, Wednesday, June 20, 2001; "Olympic Torch Route to Honor Utah Golden Boy," Bringham Young University High School, http://www.byhigh.org.
120. *Iron County Record*, September 21, 1917.
121. *Ogden (UT) Standard-Examiner*, March 8, 1924.
122. *Parowan Times*, July 26, 1925.
123. *Iron County Record*, April 28, 1916, May 16, 1913; *Parowan Times*, May 6, 1921.
124. Seegmiller, *History of Iron County*.
125. *Ninety-Fourth Annual Report, Board of Home Missions of The Presbyterian Church in The United States of America*, "Three things we need. The Holy Spirit's quickening power, ten or twelve more men, and the money to equip them."
126. *Parowan Times*, December 19, 1923; February 13, 1924.

127. Ibid., May 21, 1924; July 30, 1924.
128. Ibid., September 10, 1924.
129. Ibid., October 31, 1924; November 19, 1924; *Iron County Record*, November 6, 1924.
130. *Iron County Record*, March 27, 1925.
131. *Parowan Times*, March 18, 1925; June 23, 1926.
132. Ibid.

Chapter 14

133. *Minutes of the Rocky Mountain Faculty Athletic Conference* from archives at Utah State University in Logan and the University of Utah in Salt Lake City.
134. *Ogden Standard-Examiner*, February 26, 1926.
135. Ibid., March 6, 1926.
135. High-scoring offenses were not usual in those days.
137. *Ogden Standard-Examiner*, March 8, 1926.
138. Author's conversations with Max Worthington.
139. *Parowan Times*, September 8, 1926.

Chapter 15

140. Wylie, *Blood on the Marias*.
141. Wright, "Mormon Movement to Montana."
142. *Polk Bozeman City Directory, 1927*. Schubert Dyche lived in the Owenhouse Apartments, Unit 8. The Romneys lived at 103 Fourth Avenue, in the Bridger Arms Apartments, about 12 blocks away from the campus.
143. *Polk Bozeman City Directory, 1929, 1931*.
144. Ibid., *1931*.
145. The pond at one time had been the private spring of the Story family.
145. The Deseret Gym was torn down in 1965; the Montana State gym was remodeled and reopened at the end of 2021 as a classroom building called Romney Hall.
147. Sanderson, "Cat Thompson."
148. Frank Ward and Ashworth Thompson transcripts.

Chapter 16

149. *Exponent*, November 2, 1926; December 7, 1926; December 12, 1926.
150. *Montanan* 1927 yearbook.
151. *Exponent*, January 4, 1927.
152. Ibid., December 18, 1926.
153. *Montanan* 1927 yearbook; *Exponent*, various editions.
154. *Ogden Standard-Examiner*, January 16, 1927.
155. *Salt Lake City Tribune*, January 22, 1927.
156. *1927–1928–1929 Basketball Season Records*, Montana State University Department of Athletics.
157. Ibid.; *Denver Post*, March 13, 1927.
158. *Exponent*, March 15, 1927.
159. Sanderson, "Cat Thompson."

Chapter 17

160. Billings Senior High School yearbook, class of 1927.
161. Author's conversations with Doug Worthington. "Lon" was preferred.
162. *Nebraska State Journal* (Lincoln, NE), November 17, 1905. Worthington family religion, from discussion with Doug Worthington.
163. Lon was a manager and accountant for the Yegen Brothers department store, the largest in that part of the state.
164. Conversations with Max Wortington and Doug Worthington.
165. *Special Souvenir Issue, Eighth Annual National Interscholastic Tournament*, University of Chicago, final edition, 1925.
166. *Exponent*, March 15, 1927. Max Worthington's college decision from author's conversations with Doug Worthington.
167. Max Worthington was born in Billings on October 7, 1909.

Chapter 18

168. MSU Athletic Department Records, courtesy of Bill Lamberty.
169. Rydell, et al., *In the People's Interest*.
170. *Great Falls (MT) Tribune*, March 12, 1928.
171. Author discussions with Max Worthington.
172. *1927–1928–1929 Basketball Season Records*.

173. *Billings Gazette*, December 24, 1927.
174. *1927–1928–1929 Basketball Season Records*.
175. *Bozeman (MT) Courier*, December 30, 1927.
176. Atkinson to Eustis, October 21, 1924, MSU Special Collections, Atkinson File.
177. *1927–1928–1929 Basketball Season Records*.
178. Ibid.
179. *Billings Gazette*, December 30, 1927.
180. *Anaconda Standard*, December 31, 1927.
181. *1927–1928–1929 Basketball Season Records*.
182. *Great Falls Tribune*, January 5, 1928; January 6, 1928.
183. Ibid., January 8, 1928.
184. *Independent Record* (Helena, MT), January 12, 1928.
185. *Billings Gazette*, January 13, 1928.
186. *Great Falls Tribune*, January 17, 1926; *1927–1928–1929 Basketball Season Records*.
187. Author's observations of players in the 1940s and conversations with Max and Doug Worthington.

Chapter 19

188. *Ogden Standard-Examiner*, January 19, 1928; February 20, 1928.
189. *Statesman Journal* (Salem, OR), January 21, 1928; *1927–1928–1929 Basketball Season Records*; BYU 43–41, January 20, 1928; BYU 43–37, January 21, 1928.
190. *1927–1928–1929 Basketball Season Records*.
191. Ibid.
192. *Great Falls Tribune*, February 1, 1928.
193. Oddly, that same edition of the *Great Falls Tribune* featured a collage of the starting Bobcat players that included Peck McFarland and Ott Gardner, along with Cat Thompson, Frank Ward and Brick Breeden.
194. *Great Falls Tribune*, February 4, 1928. Utah 46–38, February 3, 1928, Bozeman; Utah 33–22, February 4, 1928, Bozeman.
195. *Independent Record*, February 8, 1928; *Independent Record*, February 5, 1928; *Billings Gazette*, February 5, 1928.
196. *Great Falls Tribune*, January 29, 1928.
197. *Billings Gazette*, February 17, 1928.
198. *Anaconda Standard*, January 19, 1928.

199. *Student Life* (Logan, UT), February 23, 1928. Max Worthington's frozen toes injury from author's conversations with Doug Worthington.
200. Ibid.; *1927–1928–1929 Basketball Season Records*.
201. *Great Falls Tribune*, February 25, 1928.
202. *1927–1928–1929 Basketball Season Records*.
203. *Great Falls Tribune*, March 12, 1928.
204. *Independent Record*, March 12, 1928; March 14, 1928; March 16, 1928.
205. Telegram from Joe Ottenheimer to Cat Thompson, March 23, 1928, from Provo, Utah, copy in Sanderson newspaper clippings file.
206. Cleveland newspaper, March 24, 1928. Sanderson Newspaper Collection: Intercollegiate—Pennsylvania; Eastern Sectional Conference—Pittsburgh; Western Conference—Purdue and Indiana; Southern—Mississippi; Southwestern—Arkansas; Missouri Valley—Oklahoma; Rocky Mountain—Montana State; Pacific Coast—Southern California; Service championship—Navy.
207. *Great Falls Tribune*, March 17, 1928.

Chapter 20

208. *Ogden Standard-Examiner*, March 24, 1928.
209. *1927–1928–1929 Basketball Season Records*.
210. *Great Falls Tribune*, March 17, 1928.
211. *Bozeman Courier*, December 30, 1927.
212. From conversations with the author's father, Paul Wylie Sr., who was present in Bozeman at the time.
213. *Ogden Standard-Examiner*, March 14, 1928.
214. Ibid., April 18, 1928; March 24, 1928.
215. Schubert Dyche's reticence, from the author's conversation with Dyche's nephew Steven Dyche.
216. Author's conversations with Max Worthington regarding Schubert Dyche.
217. "Swim Meet Is Run Off," *Daily Utah Chronicle*, May 10, 1927; "Divide Doubleheader," *Salt Lake Tribune*, February 28, 1925.
218. *Salt Lake City Tribune*, June 14, 1927. On June's swimming and diving, see *Salt Lake Tribune*, May 10, 1927.
219. From Atkinson and Montana State University Faculty Files at Montana State University Library Special Collections; *Salt Lake City Telegram*, June 14, 1927; "Playground Program Is Arranged," *Havre (MT) Daily News*, Wednesday June 29, 1927.

220. Atkinson and MSU Faculty Files, Swingle to Atkinson, April 4, 1928. The author's father was a signer on the petition to keep Dyche.
221. Notes on Schubert Dyche, Dyche Faculty File, MSU Special Collections.
222. *Anaconda Standard*, May 15, 1927.
223. Census records for 1930 show that Schubert June Dyche lived in Salt Lake City at the home of his uncle Joseph Winward, thirty, and his aunt Venetia Winward, twenty-eight. Census records, Ancestry.com.
224. After June Dyche died, Schubert married Lillian Lutes on November 8, 1930. The marriage lasted until December 31, 1957, when Lillian divorced Schubert, alleging extreme cruelty, a statutory ground of divorce at the time. Montana Divorce or Annulment Certificate, Case No. 10338.
225. 1930 Census Records, Ancestry.com.

Chapter 21

226. "Bobcat Athletic Traditions," Montana State University, https://montana.edu.
227. *Exponent*, September 26, 1928.
228. Ibid., September 28, 1928.
229. Ibid., October 2, 1928.
230. Ibid., September 9 and October 2, 1928; September 28, 1928; and September 28, 1928.
231. Ibid., September 28, 1928; November 2, 1928; September 28, 1928; and October 2, 1928.
232. Ibid.; *Montanan* 1929 yearbook.
233. Author's conversation with Steven Dyche.

Chapter 22

234. Wright, "Mormon Movement to Montana."
235. *Exponent*, November 28, 1926.
236. Author's conversations with Doug Worthington, and a review of the Rocky Mountain Faculty Athletic Conference records, ACC, 79, University of Utah Archives.
237. *Montanan* 1929 yearbook.
238. *1927–1928–1929 Basketball Season Records*.

Chapter 23

239. *Montana Standard* (Butte, MT), January 4, 1929.
240. Ibid.
241. Ibid. *1927–1928–1929 Basketball Season Records*.
242. *Montanan* 1929 yearbook. It was not an unexpected margin, given the small enrollment at Mines, and the heavy class loads its players had in their grueling curricula, which gave degrees only in engineering, with one degree in geology.
243. *1927–1928–1929 Basketball Season Records*.
244. Ibid.
245. Ibid.
246. *1927–1928–1929 Basketball Season Records*.
247. "The History of AAU Basketball," Active.com, January 2, 2018, https://www.active.com.
248. *Lawrence (KS) Journal-World*, August 5, 1927.
249. Ibid.
250. "Victor Holt," Wikipedia, https://en.wikipedia.org/wiki/Victor_Holt.
251. *1927–1928–1929 Basketball Season Records*.
252. *Salt Lake Telegram*, January 12, 1929; *Montana Standard*, January 12, 1929. McFarland started in place of Orland Ward and Gardner in place of Max Worthington. *Official Record of the Bobcats of Montana State College for 1927–1928–1929*.
253. Author conversations with Max Worthington.
254. *Daily Utah Chronicle* (Salt Lake City, UT), January 18, 1929; *Montana Standard*, January 12, 1929.
255. *Montanan* 1929 yearbook.
256. Sanderson newspaper collection, date of clipping, paper unknown. As far away as Wisconsin, where the journal at Madison, home of the state university, was published. *Exponent*, January 15, 1929.
257. *Montana Standard*, January 13, 1929.

Chapter 24

258. "Local Players Are Progressing," *Iron County Record*, January 12, 1929.
259. Allred, "Life and Contributions of Lee Hafen."
260. *1927–1928–1929 Basketball Season Records*.
261. Ibid.

262. Ibid.
263. *Official Record of the Bobcats of Montana State College for 1927–1928–1929*; *Montanan* 1929 yearbook.
264. *1927–1928–1929 Basketball Season Records*; *Montanan* 1929 yearbook.
265. Ibid.
266. *Official Record of the Bobcats*; *Montanan* 1929 yearbook.
267. Ibid.
268. Ibid.
269. *Ogden Standard-Examiner*, February 24, 1929.
270. *Billings Gazette*, March 23, 1929.
271. Sanderson, "Cat Thompson."
272. *Rocky Mountain News* (Denver, CO), March 26, 1929.
273. *Montanan* 1929 yearbook, page 158.

Chapter 25

274. *Montanan* 1929 yearbook, page 161.
275. *Salt Lake City Telegram*, Saturday January 12, 1929.
276. Al Warden article, *Salt Lake City Tribune*, March 15, 1929.
277. Leading scorers were Cat, 17.14 points per game; Frank, 15.6; and Orland, 10.7 for all games in the season.

Chapter 26

278. John Ashworth Thompson transcript.

Epilogue

279. Schubert Reilly Dyche, Montana divorce record, Ancestry.com.

BIBLIOGRAPHY

Books

Alder, Douglas D., and Karl F. Brooks. *A History of Washington County*. Springdale, UT: Zion Natural History Association, 2007.

Allen, Forrest C. *My Basketball Bible*. Kansas City, MO: Smith-Grieves Company, 1924.

Bradshaw, Hazel, ed. *Under Dixie Sun: A History of Washington County*. Washington County Chapter Daughters of Utah Pioneers, printed by *Garfield County News*, Panguitch, Utah, 1950.

Cooper, Myrtle E. *From Tent Town to City: A Chronological History of Billings, Montana, 1882–1935*. Billings, MT: self-published, 1981.

Dalton, Luella Adams. *History of Iron County Mission, Parowan, Utah*. Parowan: BYU Print Services, Daughters of the Utah Pioneers, Parowan Old Rock Church Museum, 2001.

Gerlach, Larry R. *Alma Richards: Olympian*. Salt Lake City: University of Utah Press, 2016.

Grant, Heber J. *Teachings of the Presidents of the Church*. Salt Lake City, UT: The Church of Jesus Christ of Latter-day Saints, 2002.

Hill, Bob, and Randall Baron. *The Amazing Basketball Book: The First 100 Years*. Full Court Press, a Division of Latter-day Saints, Copyright Intellectual Reserve, 2002.

Malone, Michael, Richard Roeder and William Lang. *Montana: A History*. Seattle: University of Washington Press, 1976.

Bibliography

Polk Bozeman City Directory. Various years. Bozeman, Montana.

Poll, Richard D., ed. "The Rise of the Mormon Kingdom of God." Chap. 6 in *Utah's History*. Logan: Utah State University Press, 1989.

Reeve, W. Paul. "A Little Oasis in the Desert: Community Building in Hurricane, Utah, 1860–1930" (1994). Theses and Dissertations, No. 5065, Brigham Young University, Provo, Utah. https://scholarsarchive.byu.edu/etd/5065.

Roberts, Randy. *Jack Dempsey, the Manassa Mauler*. Champaign: University of Illinois Press, 2003.

Romney, E.L. *"Dick." The Dick Romney Story*. Salt Lake City, UT: Deseret Book Company, 1965.

Romney, G. Ott. *Off the Job Living: A Modern Concept of Recreation and Its Place in the Postwar World*. New York: A.S. Barnes and Company, 1945.

Rydell, Robert, Jeffrey Safford and Pierce Mullen. *In the People's Interest: A Centennial History of Montana State University*. Bozeman: Montana State University Foundation, 1992, 27.

Seegmiller, Janet Burton. *A History of Iron County: Community above Self*. Salt Lake City: Utah State Historical Society, Iron County Commission, 1998, 228, 274.

Sheltra, Patrick. "The Romney Brothers: Utah's First Family of Sports." Chap. 52 in *100 Things Utes Fans Should Know and Do before They Die*. Chicago: Triumph Books, 2011.

Smith, Phyllis T. *Bozeman and the Gallatin Valley: A History*. Lanham, MD: TwoDot, 1996.

Webb, Ruby, comp. *A Brief History of the La Verkin Hot Springs and the La Verkin Canal*. Salt Lake City: Daughters of Utah Pioneers, Hurricane Heritage Park Museum, 1986.

Wylie, Paul R. *Blood on the Marias: The Baker Massacre*. Norman: University of Oklahoma Press, 2016.

Theses and Dissertations

Allred, Douglas V. "The Life and Contributions of Lee Hafen to Athletics at Dixie College." 1968. Utah State University, Graduate Theses and Dissertations Paper No. 2858.

MacAlduff, William H. "A History of the Health, Physical Education and Recreation Department at Montana State University, 1893–1979." Thesis for Master of Science in Physical Education, August 1979.

Bibliography

Reeve, W. Paul, "A Little Oasis in the Desert: Community Building in Hurricane, Utah, 1860–1930." 1994. Theses and Dissertations, No. 5065, Brigham Young University, Provo, Utah. https://scholarsarchive.byu.edu/etd/5065.

Wright, Julie A. "Mormon Movement to Montana." 2004. Graduate Student Theses, Dissertations & Professional Papers, No. 5596. https://scholarworks.umt.edu/etd/5596.

College Transcripts

John Ashworth Thompson, Transcript, Registrar's Office, Montana State University.

George Ottinger Romney Transcript, Office of the Registrar, Montana State University.

Schubert Reilly Dyche, transcript courtesy Registrar's Office, Montana State University.

Frank Ward Transcripts, Montana State University Registrar's office.

Sound Recordings

Sanderson, Devon, sound recording, "Cat Thompson, All American 1927, 28, 29 & 30 Montana State College, John Ashworth 'Cat' Thompson Interview," February 1974.

Newspapers

Billings (MT) Gazette
Carbondalian (Carbondale, KS)
Christian Science Monitor
Daily Herald (Provo, UT)
Deseret News (Salt Lake City, UT)
Exponent (Montana State College)
Iron County Record (Cedar City, UT)
Kansas Farmer and Mail and Breeze (Topeka, KS)
Ogden (UT) Standard
Parowan (UT) Times

Bibliography

Ronan (MT) Pioneer
Salt Lake City (UT) Telegram
Salt Lake Tribune (Salt Lake City, UT)
Topeka (KS) Daily Capital

College Yearbooks

Coloradoan, University of Colorado Yearbook, 1919.
Montanan, 1917 Montana State College Yearbook, numerous volumes.
Montanan, 1923 Montana State College yearbook, page 75.

Websites

Ancestry.com.
Encyclopedia.com. "Basketball." https://www.encyclopedia.com.
"The Great Depression Transforms Montana." http://svcalt.mt.gov/education/textbook/chapter18/Chapter18.pdf.
Wikipedia. "Fred W. Bennion." https://en.wikipedia.org.
"Wilson Sporting Goods Company History." Funding Universe. http://www.fundinguniverse.com.

Government Documents

Initiative 19. Montana ballot. November 2, 1920.
1917 Carsley/Gilbert Campus Plan, Section 7 page 12.
United States Department of the Interior. National Park Service. National Register of Historic Places. Montana State University Historic District. Montana State University, 1965.
———. National Register of Historic Places Registration Form 10-900, Montana State University Historic District OMB No. 1024-0018.

BIBLIOGRAPHY

Archives and Libraries

Brigham Young University Library Archives
Cedar City, Utah Historical Society
Dixie State University Library Archives
Montana State Historical Library. Helena, Montana.
Montana State University Library Special Collections Arcives
Parowan High School Library (Parowan, Utah)
Parowan Library Archival Collections
Southern Utah University Library Archives
St. George, Utah Historical Society
University of Utah Library Archives
Utah State University Library Archives

INDEX

A

Alhambra Athletic Club 62
All-Americans 11, 112
Allen, Forrest "Phog" 49, 53
Amateur Athletic Union (AAU) 124
Anaconda Copper Company 35
Ashland Manufacturing Company 49
Atchison, Topeka and Santa Fe Railway 44
Atkinson, Alfred 21, 28, 39, 40, 41, 55, 59, 60, 76, 81, 112, 115, 116

B

Beatrice, Nebraska 90
Beaver, Utah 66
Beherent's Billings All-Star Club 97
Bennion, Fred 25, 28, 29, 33
Billings High School 32, 35, 36, 52, 90
Bozeman Carnegie Library 39
Bozeman High School 57, 58
Branch Agricultural College (BAC) 21, 70, 72, 73, 75, 82, 107
Breeden, Bill 9
Breeden, John William "Brick" 9, 10, 56, 58, 60, 62, 63, 64, 84, 85, 86, 87, 89, 90, 94, 100, 107, 119, 121, 123, 126, 128, 131, 132, 133, 134, 135, 136, 139, 143, 153
Breeden, Ruth 9
Breeden, Tom 9
Brigham Young University 25, 54, 112
Brothers Bank 85
BYU Cougars 11, 108, 117, 132
BYU Junior College 73

C

Cache Valley 20

Index

California AAU league 62
Carpenter, Clyde 92
Carroll College (called Mt. Saint Charles College at the time) 87, 106, 134
Cedar City, Utah 10, 21, 22, 67, 68, 69, 70, 72, 73, 75
Chauner, W.F. 57
Cheyenne, Wyoming 77
Christian Scientist 90
Colorado College 87
Colorado Fuel and Iron Company (CF&I) 45
Colorado State Teachers 98, 123
Comanche 45
Communism 83
Conron, Eliza 44
Cook Paint Company 114, 122, 124
Cornell University 66, 116
County Fair in Cedar City 67
Cox, Lorraine 130, 131
Custer, George Armstrong 45

D

Dempsey, Jack 46, 105, 148
Deseret Gym 25, 31, 33, 41, 47, 53, 67, 81, 85, 107, 121, 135
Disciples of Christ denomination 98
Dixie Academy, St. George 18
Dixie College, St. George, Utah. *See* junior colleges
Dixie Flyers 73, 74
Dixie Normal College, St. George 18
Dow, Peter 86
Drill Hall 31, 41
Dyche, Alexander 44
Dyche, Edward 45, 47
Dyche, Eliza 45
Dyche, June 114, 115, 134, 155
Dyche, Lewis 45
Dyche, Lillian 144
Dyche, Schubert June 13, 21, 37, 38, 44, 45, 47, 49, 51, 55, 61, 72, 75, 77, 78, 82, 87, 89, 100, 112, 114, 115, 117, 119, 120, 121, 125, 126, 127, 128, 131, 132, 135, 140, 143, 147, 151, 154
Dyche, Schubert Reilly 44

E

East High School of Salt Lake City, Utah 33, 36, 38, 44, 51, 116, 150
eligibility 21, 26, 29, 73, 75, 78, 82, 121
Elks Club of Bozeman 139, 144
El Segundo, California 71

F

Fairview, Montana 57
Fitchburg Academy 91
Forsythe, Montana 54
Fort Bayard, New Mexico 48
Fort Ellis, Montana 39
from the sticks 20

INDEX

G

Gallatin Valley, Montana 52, 80
gandy dancer 77
GB&Q Railway Company 97
Gibbons, Tommy 105
Glynne, Marty 10
Glynne, Vallery "Val" 10, 84, 95, 150
Goates, Les 102
Golden Bobcats 92, 127, 132, 137, 139, 173
Grant, Heber J. 13, 17
Greater University of Montana 111
Great Falls All-Stars 136
Great Falls High School 57
Great Salt Lake Valley, Utah 24, 52
Great War 32, 35
Green Front Grocery 45
Green, Mary Esther 68, 69, 71
gunfire incident 96

H

Hagerstown, Maryland 92
Hamilton Hall 27, 40, 81
Hamilton, James 27
Harding, Ruth 36
Hartwig, Adolph 54, 55, 60, 62, 63
Harvard University 26
Havre All-Stars 136
Hec Edmundson Pavilion 85
Helena, Montana 79, 87, 95, 106, 134, 153
Helms Foundation 52
Holt, Vic 125, 126, 127, 128, 129

Hunter, Lynn 69
Hurricane, Utah 13, 14, 15, 16, 18

I

Idaho Falls, Idaho 79
Idaho State College 62
Idaho Technical College 62
Intermountain Association of the Amateur Athletic Union (AAU) 30
Irish Catholics 80, 119
Iron County, Utah 67, 68, 70, 130

J

Jamestown University 85
Judd, Kate 14
junior colleges 73, 77, 82, 84

K

Kansas University, Lawrence, Kansas 45

L

La Rochelle, France 46
Latter-day Saints 17, 25, 47
Laverkin, Utah 10, 94
LDS College, Logan, Utah. *See* junior colleges
LaSelle, Mary 90
Lewis Hall 41
Little Big Horn battlefield 45

167

INDEX

Livingston 36
Livingston, Montana 36
Livingston Railway Club 96
Long Beach Athletic Club 62
Loyola College 62

M

Massachusetts Institute of
    Technology (MIT) 27
"M," block letter 28, 117
McFarland, Gilbert "Peck" 72, 97,
    98, 99, 106, 153, 156
McGough, John 111
Meenan, Dan 64
Milford Athletic Club 77
Milford, Utah 77
Missouri River 40, 56
Mongolia (steamship) 46
Monida Pass 100, 107
Montana Hall 40, 41, 59, 76, 81, 82
Montana Normal School, Dillon,
    Montana 62
Montanan yearbook 30, 56, 102,
    111, 119, 140
Montana State College
  Montana State College of
      Agriculture and Mechanical
      Arts (MSC) 13, 22, 23, 27,
      28, 29, 31, 38, 40, 43, 44, 51,
      54, 56, 57, 59, 71, 72, 80, 81,
      83, 86, 88, 91, 95, 103, 111,
      116, 130, 148, 173
Montana State School of Mines,
    Butte, Montana 62
Montana State University 10, 27,
    43, 73, 86, 100, 148
Mormon pioneers 14, 24
Mormon Temple 15, 47
Moscow, Idaho 61, 84, 117
MSC Gymnasium 41
Murdock Academy 66
musician first class 46

N

National Collegiate Champions 11
National Interscholastic
    Tournament at the University
    of Chicago 20
Naval Reserves 35
Newhouse Hotel, Salt Lake City,
    Utah 33
1912 Stockholm Olympics 66
Northern Hotel, Billings, Montana 36

O

Oklahoma State Conference 99
Oregon State Beavers 99
Ottenheimer, Joe 22, 23, 61, 79, 80
Ottinger, George M. 24, 112

P

Pacific Coast Athletic Conference 87
Palouse River 123
Parowan High School, Parowan,
    Utah 23
Peterson, Vidal 130, 135
Phillips University Haymakes, Enid,
    Oklahoma 98

INDEX

Pittsburgh University 143
Pocatello, Idaho 62
Potlach Athletic Club 85
Pratt's Bookstore AAU team 98
Presbyterians 68
Protestants 68, 80
Pueblo, Colorado 45

R

Reno, Nevada 62
rheumatic fever 120
Rhodes Scholarship 29
Richards, Alma 66, 67, 77
Ricks College, Rexburg, Idaho. *See* junior colleges
Roberts Hall 40
Rocky Mountain Conference 25, 29, 41, 48, 54, 59, 60, 62, 63, 76, 84, 85, 87, 98, 102, 103, 106, 108, 110, 112, 120, 121, 129, 130, 135, 136, 137, 138
Rocky Mountain Faculty Athletic Conference. *See* Rocky Mountain Conference
Romney, Earnest Lowell "Dick" 25
Romney, Floyd 25, 54
Romney, George Ottinger "Ott" 11, 21, 23, 24, 27, 29, 30, 32, 33, 35, 36, 37, 44, 49, 50, 51, 52, 54, 55, 58, 59, 60, 62, 63, 72, 74, 75, 77, 78, 80, 81, 85, 87, 89, 90, 92, 93, 94, 95, 97, 99, 100, 103, 107, 111, 112, 115, 116, 117, 123, 125, 132, 133, 135, 143
Romney, George W. 25
Romney, Milton "Mitt" 25
Romney, W.W. "Woody" 25
Roscoe, St. Clair County, Missouri 56
Ryan Lab 40

S

Salem, Oregon 99
Sanderson, Devon 9
Schubert, Franz 44
Schwarzschild & Sulzberger (later Sulzberger & Son's) 49
Scott, Kim Allen 10
Seattle Amateur Athletic Club 62
Shanley, George H., Great Falls architect 40
Shelby, Montana 105
Shepherd, June 114
Sheridan All-Stars 98
Sherman, General William Tecumseh 79
Sigma Alpha Epsilon fraternity 93
Sigma Chi fraternity 26, 80, 93, 96
Snake River 79
Snow, Erastus 14
Spanish flu 35, 36
Spokane, Washington 85
Springville, Utah 68
Stagg, Amos Alonzo 25, 53, 91
Stanford University 48, 66
Stewart Park 108
St. George, Utah 14, 130, 140
St. Paul Hotel 73
Swingle, Deane 76, 115

Index

T

Tabernacle in Temple Square 47
Teetzel, C.T. 29, 30
Terry, General Alfred 79
Thompson, Dr. Elizabeth Perkes 15
Thompson, John Ashworth "Cat" 11, 15, 19, 50, 72, 75, 77, 79, 81, 82, 84, 85, 86, 87, 88, 89, 94, 95, 96, 98, 99, 100, 101, 102, 105, 106, 107, 109, 110, 112, 115, 121, 123, 124, 125, 126, 127, 129, 130, 131, 132, 133, 134, 135, 136, 137, 139, 140, 143, 145, 153
Thompson, Kate 15
Thompson, Wilford 14, 15
Toppenish Athletic Club 85
Traphagen Hall 41
Twitchell, Alvin 87

U

Union Pacific Railway 77
University of California at Berkeley 48
University of Chicago 25, 91
University of Colorado in Boulder 46
University of Denver Pioneers 98
University of Deseret 24
University of Idaho Vandals 84
University of Nevada 62
University of Oklahoma 125
University of Southern California 66
University of the Pacific 62
University of Utah 26, 27
University of Utah's Beehive Club 26
University of Washington 85
Utah State, Logan, Utah 72
Utah State tournament 20
Utah State University 10, 29
Utah Valley 20

V

Virginia City, Montana 79
Virgin River in Utah 13

W

Wakarusa, Shawnee County, Kansas 44
Walla Walla, Washington 123
Warden, Al 85, 86, 102, 139
Ward, Frank "Huzzy" 9, 10, 11, 21, 23, 66, 67, 68, 69, 70, 71, 72, 73, 74, 75, 77, 78, 81, 82, 84, 85, 86, 87, 89, 94, 96, 98, 100, 103, 105, 106, 107, 114, 121, 123, 125, 126, 127, 128, 131, 133, 134, 135, 136, 138, 143, 144, 151, 153
Ward, Hal Green 115
Ward, Jim 10, 79, 80, 144
Ward, Orland 9, 23, 65, 67, 69, 70, 78, 79, 80, 81, 82, 85, 96, 105, 106, 107, 121, 123, 126, 127, 131, 133, 134, 135, 136, 137, 138, 144, 156
Ward, Tex 9
Washington State College, Pullman, Washington 52, 61, 123

Index

Washington State Cougars 52
Weber College, Ogden, Utah. *See*
    junior colleges
Whitehead, Chester 20
Whitman College 85, 123
Wilkes Theater 33
Willard, Jess 46
Willard Weihe String Quartet 47
Williams, Ruth 47
Wilson Sporting Goods 49
Worden, Frank 58, 95, 119, 121
World Heavyweight Boxing
    Championship 46
Worthington, Doug 9
Worthington, Glenn 105
Worthington, Leonard. L. 90
Worthington, LaSelle 90
Worthington, Max 9, 90, 92, 94,
    95, 96, 97, 99, 100, 106, 107,
    119, 120, 121, 123, 126, 127,
    128, 131, 132, 133, 134, 135,
    136, 139, 152, 153, 156
Wylie, Harold "Gus" 10, 57
Wyoming University 102

Y

Yakima, Washington YMCA 85
YMCA 32, 103
Young, Brigham 14, 24

ABOUT THE AUTHOR

Paul R. Wylie lives in Bozeman, Montana, the home in 1929 of the Golden Bobcats at Montana State College. His father and his aunts and uncles attended MSC in the 1920s, and the family knew the players, many as family friends. Growing up, Wylie heard many firsthand reports of their exploits. The author himself graduated from MSC in 1959 with a degree in chemical engineering, which he followed with a law degree in 1965 from American University in Washington, D.C. After he retired from his career as an intellectual property rights attorney, he set about researching and writing history. Paul is the author of *The Irish General: Thomas Francis Meagher* (2007) and *Blood on the Marias: The Baker Massacre* (2016), published by the University of Oklahoma Press.